CANYONING
CLASSIC CANYONS IN SPAIN, FRANCE AND ITALY

About the Author

John has been climbing, walking and mountaineering for over 30 years. He grew up on the fringes of the Lake District and has since travelled extensively to the mountain and crag areas of Europe, North America, and other parts of the world. He has climbed in about 30 countries and contributed to several rock-climbing guides, and descended his first canyon in the Sierra de Guara in 1992. He was astonished to find that this completely unfamiliar activity seemed at least as much fun as climbing.

CANYONING
CLASSIC CANYONS IN SPAIN, FRANCE AND ITALY

by
John Bull

2 POLICE SQUARE, MILNTHORPE, CUMBRIA LA7 7PY
www.cicerone.co.uk

First edition 2008
ISBN-13: 978-1-85284-508-7

A catalogue record for this book is available from the British Library.

DEDICATIONS

To anyone I've shared a day down a canyon with: thanks. And to Bob Hamilton, Graham Hufton and Derek L Walker, without whom none of this may ever have happened.

SPECIAL THANKS

To Jess and Kieran, for the fun parts.

DISCLAIMER

The canyons in this guide can be descended in safety most of the time, using the information presented in this guidebook. However, canyoning involves many dangers. There is no substitute for experience and self-sufficiency in the outdoors, familiarity with changing conditions, and experience in rope handling and being in water.

There is every reason to limit your ambitions depending on your ability to abseil and your ability to swim. It is no exaggeration to say that your life may depend on expertise in both of these activities. Learn them elsewhere.

Except insofar as such liability cannot be excluded by law, the author, publisher and distributors do not accept any liability for injury or damage caused to, or by, canyoners, third parties, or property arising from the guidebook's use.

The decision to descend a canyon is entirely yours and you do so at your own risk.

Front cover: In the Barranco del Infierno (Route 18) (photo: The Orange House)

Back cover: One of several small falls in the narrows of the Ravin de Notre Dame (Route 33)

CONTENTS

PREFACE 10

INTRODUCTION 13
The region and its wildlife...13
Seasons and when to go..18
Getting there and local transport 20
Preparations and what to take...22
Using this guide 24

TECHNICAL ASPECTS OF CANYON DESCENT 25
Route grading and quality...25
Safety precautions..26
Team size...27
Equipment and clothing..28
Some techniques..35
Special considerations in aquatic canyons 44

THE CANYONS
SPAIN
SIERRA DE GUARA...49
Practicalities 51

The Routes...56
Rio Vero area...56
1. Rio Vero...56
2. Barranco de Basender...59
3. Barranco de Portiacha...61
4. Barranco de Chimiachas..62
5. Barranco de Fornocal..63
6. Barranco de las Palomeras 64

Rodellar area 67
7. Barranco de Mascún Superior 67
8. Barranco de Otín 71
9. Barranco de Mascún Inferior 74
10. Barranco de Mascún Inferior – last section...................................77
11. Gorgas Negras 79

12. Garganta de Barrasil 80
13. Garganta de la Peonara Superior..82
14. Garganta de la Peonara Inferior 84
15. Oscuros de Balcés..86
16. Estrechos de Balcés...87
17. Rio Formiga – Barranco de Yara..90

COSTA BLANCA 91
Practicalities 93

The routes 98
18. Barranco del Infierno 99
19. Barranc del Sant/Barranco de Melo....................................102
20. Barranc de l'Estret de Penyes..105
21. Barranco de Soler 108
22. Barranco de les Raboses 112
23. Barranco de Relleu 113

MALLORCA 117
Practicalities 117

The routes 122
24. Torrente de Pareis...122
25. Torrente de Gorg Blau et Sa Fosca 126
26. Other canyons in the Sierra de Tramuntana.........................128

FRANCE..130
HAUTE-PROVENCE 130
Practicalities 133

The routes 139
Apt and the Vaucluse area..139
27. Gorges de Véroncle 139
28. Gorges d'Opodette 144
29. Grand Vallot d'Opodette..146

Sisteron area 149
30. Gorges du Valbelle..149

Moustiers-Ste-Marie area 153
31. Ravin du Balène...153
32. Ravin de Riou 156
33. Ravin de Notre Dame 158

34. Ravin de Vénascle...161
35. Ravin d'Angouire 164
Verdon area...166
36. Verdon Gorge – upper section...168
37. Verdon Gorge – middle section...,,,,,,171
38. Verdon Gorge side-canyons: Mainmorte, Font de Barbin,
    Ferne, Cabrielle...173
39. Le Baou 176
40. L'Artuby 177

ITALY 178
Sᴀʀᴅɪɴɪᴀ 178
Practicalities 178
The routes 183
41. Codula Fuili..183
42. Golade Gorropu 186
43. Riu Fluminedde and Golade Gorropu 189
44. Codula Orbisi...191
45. Badde Pentumas...192

Appendix 1: Glossary 195
Appendix 2: Notes on Corsica 197
Appendix 3: Insurance, accidents and rescue.............................198
Appendix 4: Accidents and first aid basics 199
Appendix 5: Canyons by grade and a 'top six' 200
Appendix 6: Route summary table 202

Map Key

————————————	road
– – – – – – – –	route described
· · · · · · · · · · · · · · · ·	alternative route
●●●●●●●●●●●●●●●●	footpath
– – – – – – –	canyon/section of route
————————————	ravine
▪ ▪ ▪ ▪ ▪ ▪ ▪ ▪ ▪ ▪	dirt road
~~	river, sea or lake
· · · · · · · · · · · · · · · ·	dry stream
▪ ▪ ▪ ▪ ▪ ▪ ▪ ▪ ▪ ▪	river bed
▪ ▪ ▪ ▪ ▪ ▪ ▪ ▪ ▪ ▪	border
●	town/village
●	major town
▪	building
▲	peak
♁	church or chapel
Å	campsite
①	route number
🚶	start
🚶	finish
🚶	start/finish
©	cave
⛴	ferry
⌣	col
🅿	parking
//	abseil (in profiles)
⌂	bridge
←	general direction arrow
←	route direction arrow
🌳	wooded area

Regions covered
in this book

PREFACE

Canyoning, the descent of natural gorges, is a spicy mix of all good things adventur-ous. In a canyon, you are transported away from your familiar environment to a new world. You're a temporary visitor, passing through with a one-way ticket – you follow a defined geographical feature, often inescapable for several kilometres, on a journey into the unknown. Even an easy, dry canyon can be very atmospheric, with dramatic, high walls enclosing a narrow channel and little scope for immediate escape. Add a rush of noisy water, a committing abseil or two, and you have an exhilarating envi-ronment. Only at the bottom do you, once more, join the familiar world.

The mountain and coastal areas of Southern Europe are home to a host of canyons, many of which offer superb and unique experiences. Canyoning in Europe is a mix-and-match of hiking, scrambling, swimming and abseiling – a mixture not readily available in the British Isles, where there are no full-scale gorges and there is little in the way of truly dramatic mountain limestone scenery. As a result, canyoning is a relatively unknown activity to most UK outdoor enthu-siasts. (It's not the same as ghyll scrambling – in canyoning you go down, not up.)

So, what's it like? Well, as with a day's climbing or scrambling in the moun-tains, you have a growing sense of anticipation during the walk-in, the feeling of progressing into unknown rugged terrain on the route itself, the relaxation of the walk-out and a sense of fulfilment at the end of the day. You also have the freedom of fast movement and the pleasure of discovering what's around the next corner. Canyoning has been described as outdoor caving but that doesn't do it justice – it's much better than that! If you want to try something a little different for a few days or weeks, or merely want a change in the middle of your climbing or walk-ing holiday, why not give it a go?

If you've never canyoned before, fear not: some of the easier canyons are fairly straightforward gorge walks. Although they do range enormously in diffi-culty and commitment from two-hour strolls to serious multi-day aquatic expedi-tions, each of the areas in this book has a preponderance of easier rather than harder canyons and a natural bias towards the lower end of the difficulty scale.

However, confidence in water will make a difference to the level of your enjoyment in an aquatic canyon. A wetsuit will do much to allay any fears. Many canyons can be done just with one-piece 'Farmer Johns' or a shortie-style wetsuit, although you may be more comfortable in a full suit. If you've never worn one before you will be amazed at how buoyant you become. In fact, the buoyancy afforded by a full wetsuit makes it almost impossible to swim properly or quickly, and the most effective stroke seems to be a sort of slow motion doggy-paddle. Let this tell you something: it's best sometimes just to go with the flow. Few things can

Canyoning country – the Sierra de Guara

be more peaceful than floating on your back, effortlessly drifting downstream, with huge canyon walls above you and distant black shapes of soaring vultures overhead – a river cruise where you are the boat as well as the passenger.

The more technical expeditions invariably include abseiling and scrambling. An ability to abseil will open up options to undertake many more canyons, often with much more dramatic situations. With a rope, harness, a few slings and karabiners you're in possession of a complete set of kit for dry canyoning, and, as most canyons that require abseil descents are feasible with a single rope of 50m, climbers will not need to buy any extra gear. Ideally, you should perfect your abseiling skills *before* venturing into a canyon. But the friendly nature of the Southern European canyons makes them suitable places to learn and this guide provides a basic grounding in techniques and skills (see 'Technical aspects of canyon descent'). In any case, any team with a basic level of experience of abseiling and scrambling should be able to have a go at the easier canyons in this guide.

Needless to say, there is much competition amongst canyon explorers and a first descent is a coveted prize. European canyoning activists are true explorers and many pioneers have equipped hundreds of gorges with abseil stations and the occasional fixed rope or cable. This means that you will never need to drill a bolt hole or spend money on hardware such as chains and cables that you then leave behind for any of the canyons in this guide. It also means that you are following in the footsteps of others, which the more pioneering may find a little dissatisfying. More serious fare awaits them in the colder water and higher altitudes of the Alps and the Pyrenees, and there are many hundreds of new canyons waiting to be discovered in far-flung parts of the globe. Go to it!

John Bull, 2008

11

The final cascade, Barranc de l'Estret de Penyes (Route 20)

INTRODUCTION

The areas in this guide – the Sierra de Guara in the foothills of the Pyrenees, the hills of the Costa Blanca, Mallorca, Haute-Provence and Sardinia – are predominantly limestone uplands, clustered around the western end of the Mediterranean. (The general area is shown in the overview map.) These regions are pleasantly sunny for much of the year and, with the help of budget flight operators, many climbers, walkers, cavers and cyclists now make annual visits, alongside the hordes of beachgoers. For active Brits wanting a quick escape to warmer climes, new areas are opening up all the time and an increasing number of walking and climbing guides has hit the book-shelves in recent years.

This book, however, is the first canyoning guide to these 'great escape' destinations, and with this in mind, it is intended to be introductory and wide-ranging, rather than a defin-itive catalogue of the hundreds of canyoning routes in this huge area. Nevertheless, you will find enough information here to enjoy anything from a single day's canyoning within a walking or climbing holiday to a full-scale canyoning trip lasting a week or two.

Canyons range from the massive and inspiring to the modest and intri-cate, and their variety is an endless source of fascination. Each area offers its special experiences, whether you are in the big wilderness country of the Guara in the Pyrenees or Verdon in Provence, or absorbed in the detail of an enclosed corridor on the Costa Blanca (an area where you might not have expected to find canyon wilder-ness!). Sardinia and Mallorca have an island feel, characterised by big days and long, committing descents, but here, too, there are spectacular easy gorges that don't require abseiling or scrambling. In all of these areas, regardless of their grandeur, you will also find the tiniest of passageways and the most bijou of features. Whatever your inclination, the Sierra de Guara, Costa Blanca, Mallorca, Provence and Sardinia have all the canyoning bases covered.

This introductory section provides some background to the areas and useful information on how to get there and when to go. The next section offers advice on techniques and equipment and a reminder of some of the canyoning basics.

THE REGION AND ITS WILDLIFE

The landscape of Southern Europe is one of contrasts: clumps of shrubs and other hardy vegetation, acres of exposed rock, lush areas of forest and idyllic glades. Hand-in-hand with this goes the weather – one minute the midday sun parches the arid land, and the next the landscape is dominated by black skies and dramatic hail-storms – but the sun is never far away.

With one or two exceptions in the pre-Pyrenean area of the Sierra de Guara, where underlying conglomerate strata have been exposed to the cutting action of streams and rivers, the canyons in this guide are composed of limestone, represented in all its hues from bright white through sombre greys and blues to deep orange. Throughout the areas, on a hot day, you are bound to see several varieties of lizards, and perhaps a gecko or two, as well as large insects such as crickets and cicadas, the scene enhanced by an abundance of wild flowers and shrubs throughout the year.

Sierra de Guara

In the Sierra de Guara, a collision between Mediterranean and Atlantic climatic zones leads to a diversity of local animal and plant populations. Higher slopes of sparse brush give way to more humid forests of pine, followed by oaks and juniper trees on the southern slopes.

A few determined rivers cut through the southern expanses of limestone and conglomerate, forming steep-sided gorges with dramatic rock formations at Vadiello, Salto de Roldan, Mascún (Routes 7–10) and Riglos. As they have travelled towards the plain over millions of years, the rivers Alcanadre, Mascún, Isuala and Vero have modelled the landscape spectacularly.

The Guara canyons form an extensive habitat for wildlife, including trout, river crab and the Pyrenean newt. The cliffs are colonised with specialised plants, including some that are unique to the area. Stands of Portuguese oak woods, holm-oak woods, thick arbutus copses, mastic trees, juniper trees and box trees populate the mountain slopes.

The area is also rich in birds of prey. Bearded vultures, Egyptian vultures, griffin vultures, golden eagles, hawks, eagle owls and a range of forest

LAMMERGEIERS

The bearded vulture, or Lammergeier, reputedly the world's only bone-eating (or osteophagic) bird, has an important sanctuary in the canyons of the Sierra de Guara, especially the Rio Vero (Route 1) and its side-canyons. Lammergeiers feed on marrow which they get by dropping bones repeatedly onto rocks, often in their favourite haunts or ossuaries, high on cliff ledges. The name 'bearded vulture' refers to the ochre colour of the ruff of quills around the neck, which the birds stain by rubbing in iron-rich mud. Currently the Spanish Pyrenees host over a hundred groups of these birds, about 10 per cent of which are in the Sierra de Guara, making it the densest population in Europe.

Clipping some fixed ropes in the Ravin du Balène (Route 31)

species including the booted or short-toed eagle are all resident, and a special protection area has been declared for birdlife. Migratory alpine birds such as wallcreeper or alpine accentor can be seen at close range during winter and early spring.

The Sierra de Guara is excitingly wild and the many semi-deserted villages and hamlets testify to a rural population that has grown sparser in recent decades. In 1990, the Sierra de Guara Natural Park was established to protect this area of great ecological, scientific and educational value. It covers over 80,000 hectares and encompasses parts of the Barbastro region, the Valley of Huesca, High Gállego and Sobrarbe.

Costa Blanca and Mallorca

These areas are more densely populated than the Guara, but the limestone features can be just as spectacular, notably at Calpe's Peñón de Ifach and Mallorca's Formentor peninsula. However, there is less of a sense of wilderness, as the hand of man is everywhere visible.

Spain has more varieties of wildlife than any other country in Europe, but in these areas animals are less protected and much more widely hunted. You're unlikely to see the rarer species such as wolves and lynx around these parts but you might see foxes, wild boar, ibex and wild goat. Some valleys such as the Guadalest are returning to a wild state, however, with trees now protected and many of

the agricultural terraces abandoned. There are large areas of hillside that are now inaccessible and undisturbed, including the area around the Barranco del Infierno (Route 18), and wildlife is returning.

Of Europe's bird species, 70 per cent either visit or breed in Spain, and the Formentor peninsula in Mallorca is a twitcher's heaven. Close to here (Routes 24–26) you can expect to see honey buzzards, black kites, booted eagles and Mallorca's own bird of prey, Eleanora's falcon. Other wildlife thriving here include swifts, martins, bats and the ubiquitous small lizards.

Haute-Provence

The enormous cliffs of the Verdon Gorge (Routes 36 and 37) form Europe's most dramatic expression of the erosive power of flowing water. The course of the Verdon river takes it though limestone country as it descends from the Maritime Alps to emerge abruptly into the dammed Lac de Sainte Croix. The gorge and lake are in the Verdon Regional Natural Park, and there has been a successful programme over the last few years to reintroduce wildlife such as golden eagles and the huge griffon vultures, which can frequently be seen soaring above the mountains or down into the gorge. In the Luberon and Apt areas you won't see these great birds, but black kite and common buzzards are often seen hovering about in fine weather.

Limestone + water = erosion and, eventually, a canyon

In April, acacia trees are covered with fragrant white blossoms and masses of wild irises add colour, while in May yellow broom covers the mountains and lines the roadside. Wild flowers – such as the purple columbine, sweet peas and many varieties of orchid – abound.

Sardinia

Sardinia's landscape is a varied mix of mountain massifs and plateaux in the north contrasting with the Campidano plain across the south. The east coast is rich in bays (Route 41) and caves (Route 45) and is characterised by extraordinary rocky formations. The most common vegetation is Mediterranean *maquis*, comprising evergreen bushes and shrubs (such as lavender, thyme, myrtle and rosemary myrtle, lentisk, laurel, mastic and oleander) dotted about the arid landscape. There are also holm-oaks, oaks and cork-oaks, as well as olive groves and prickly pears.

Sardinia has been separated from the European mainland for millions of years, and several endemic animal species have evolved that are smaller than their mainland relatives (an evolutionary trend known as island nanism), such as the small wild horses of the Giara plateau and the Sardinian deer.

Peregrine hawks can sometimes be spotted, and, in summer and winter, ponds in the southern and central part of the island are visited by pink flamingos migrating between Tunisia

17

Reptiles huddling for warmth in a Provencal canyon

A tick – check your body daily for relatives of this specimen

and the Camargue (several migrant colonies can be seen at the Molentargius pond near Cagliari, and in pools in the Oristano area). The national park in the Gennargentu mountains is home to wild pigs, wild-cats, Sardinian deer, falcons, golden eagles, mouflon (wild sheep), kites, black vultures and bearded vultures. There are also many different birds along the coasts and on the small islands offshore, where, if you are lucky, you might see turtles, dolphins and the very rare monk seal.

The National Archaeological Museum of Cagliari contains prehistoric tombs and other significant artefacts from the Punic and Roman periods, and the Sardinian landscape is peppered with interesting constructions from the ancient Nuragic civilisation. These stone structures include the remains of whole villages and are unique to Sardinia.

SEASONS AND WHEN TO GO

The sunny, mild climate means that any time of year is good for canyoning in the Mediterranean areas. An overview is given here, with much more detail within each area section.

There are year-round canyoning options in all of the five areas except Verdon, where there is snow in winter. As a general rule, aquatic conditions are best in spring and early summer, but there are plenty of dry canyoning opportunities year-round, especially in the Costa Blanca, Mallorca and Sardinia.

In the more mountainous Verdon and Guara, spring meltwater swells the rivers from the high mountains, giving plenty of noisy atmosphere and cold aquatic conditions. Summer is more comfortable in these areas, perfect for long stretches of aquatic canyoning, although the flow of water declines as the summer progresses. Good sport can be found from spring to autumn. August can be

Afloat in the Garganta de Barrasil (Route 12)

crowded but September is beautiful and quiet, and often there is still enough water for reasonable conditions. In winter, you would have to be very keen to want to venture into an aquatic canyon in the high Verdon (even if it were permitted) but canyoning in the Guara is still an option.

Most of the Costa Blanca, Sardinia and Mallorca canyons are predominantly dry year-round, and in summer they offer an escape from the heat. Some of the canyons in these areas are best in spring when some water is still flowing. Summer drought periods can turning flowing water into stagnant pools, but these are generally on the small side and are more of an inconvenience than a problem.

Rainfall and winds in the colder months can give unsettled periods in any of the areas, although you would be unlucky if this lasted for more than a few days at a stretch. If you are climbing in the Costa Blanca or Mallorca, you may even find the rainy periods are ideal for bagging a canyon or two in preference to trying to climb between showers.

GETTING THERE AND LOCAL TRANSPORT

Getting there
The five areas each have one or two airports. The table on the next page shows important local towns that you will need to aim for, and suggestions for where to base yourself. Travel

details to get to these areas are outlined here, while further local details are given in each of the five sections.

With the advent of the low-cost airlines, getting to the Med has never been easier or cheaper. Ryanair, EasyJet, BMiBaby and others offer reliable low-cost air fares and are especially cheap outside school holiday periods. Check the following sites for low-cost flights: www.easyjet.com; www.flightcomparison.co.uk; www.cheapflights.co.uk; www.ryanair.com.

Airlines
- Air Europa (0870 2401 501)
- Air France (08453 591000, www.airfrance.co.uk)
- BA (08708 509850, www.britishairways.co.uk) bmibaby (08702 642229, www.bmibaby.co.uk)
- British Midland (0870 6070555)
- EasyJet (08717 500100, www.easyjet.com)
- Flybe (www.flybe.com)
- GB Airways (08708 509850, www.gbairways.com)
- Globespan (www.flyglobespan.com)
- Iberia Airlines (www.iberiaairlines.co.uk)
- Jet2 (08707 378282, www.jet2.com)
- Monarch (www.flymonarch.com)
- Ryanair (www.ryanair.com)
- Thomsonfly (08701 900737, www.thomsonfly.com)

Area	Airport	Nearest rail station	Main local towns/cities	Ideal base
Sierra de Guara	Barcelona	Huesca	Huesca	Rodellar
Costa Blanca	Alicante	Alicante	Benidorm, Calpe	Various
Mallorca	Palma	Sóller	Sóller	Sóller
Provence	Marseille Nice	Aix-en-Provence Manosque	Aix-en-Provence	Apt, Moustiers La Palud
Sardinia	Alghero Cágliari	-	Dorgali	Dorgali, Cala Gonone

Rail

French rail information: www.sncf.fr

Spanish rail information: http://horarios.renfe.es/hir/ingles.html

A useful rail information site is www.europeanrailguide.com, which covers the whole of Europe. For tickets, also try www.raileurope.com or www.raileurope.co.uk. Rail travel is not really a worthwhile option in Mallorca except for travelling from Palma and Sóller, which is closer to the canyoning. Similarly, the Sardinian rail network will get you from the airport at Alghero or Cágliari to Macomer in the west, but you will need further transport to get to Dorgali on the eastern side of the island.

Ferries (Corsica and Sardinia)

UK and European ferry timetable/price comparison website: www.aferry.co.uk Southern Ferries/SNCM (020 7491 4968, www.sncm.fr)

If you're touring Europe by car, useful ferry routes run from the mainland to both Corsica and Sardinia. Routes to Corsica (Calvi, Bastia, Ajaccio and Ile Rousse) operate from the French ports of Toulon and Nice and the Italian ports of Livorno and Savona, and several ferry routes are available for hopping over from Corsica to Sardinia. Direct ferries from Livorno or Rome/Civitavecchia arrive in both Ólbia and Arbatax on the east coast of Sardinia, not far from Dorgali and the canyoning. As a foot passenger, you can get from Rome to Arbatax for only about €100 return including train fares.

Car hire

A hire car is extremely useful in most of the destinations. Although it is possible to manage without, especially in the Sierra de Guara and in Provence, for Costa Blanca, Mallorca and Sardinia you do need a car. By far the simplest approach from the UK is to fly in and rent one. Easyrentacar (allied to Europcar) are good and cheap, especially if you're flying Easyjet. Car hire companies at most airports include Alamo, Avis, Budget, Hertz and Europcar. For the Costa Blanca (where car hire is as cheap as it gets), try searching on the internet for Jet Car, Holiday Autos or Sun Cars. In Sardinia, you can book Hertz car rentals from the Ryanair website at a discount. For any of the areas, try: www.rent.it or www.holidayautos.co.uk.

PREPARATIONS AND WHAT TO TAKE

Fitness and skills

Experienced rock-climbers and cavers will have no problem adjusting their skills to canyoning situations and will find canyoning well within their comfort zones. Others from, for example, a hill-walking background, may want to go on a day or weekend course in the UK to pick up abseiling and ropework skills. There are many centres in North Wales, the Lakes, the Pennines and Scotland – check the adverts in the back pages of the outdoor magazines or on the internet. The best organisations are run by qualified climbing or caving guides – look for accreditation from the Association of Mountain Instructors (AMI), Adventure Activities Licensing Authority (AALA), Association of Caving Instructors (ACI) or similar. Alternatively, join a climbing or caving club or try out your local climbing wall, many of which run basic instruction courses.

A basic level of fitness, such as that necessary for a summer fell walk, is essential, but canyoning in Southern Europe is not likely to tax your navigation, route-finding, map-reading or endurance skills to anything like the degree needed for, for example, a winter ascent of Helvellyn or the Glyders. However, some of the longer aquatic canyons can become arduous outings, especially if you lose body heat. Here, a higher level of fitness and resourcefulness is an asset.

Equipment

The equipment you need will depend on your level of ambition. Gear requirements are given at the start of each route description. Each area has canyons of a range of difficulties. Some are easy walks, but for most you will need to abseil, needing at least a rope, harness, an abseil device and a few slings for making cow's tails to clip into fixed anchors. To get the most out of the Sierra de Guara or Verdon, you will also need a wetsuit. (These are easily rented in the Guara.)

Codula Fuili – the main (third) pitch (Route 41)

Maps

Sierra de Guara
- Michelin road map 443
- Editorial Alpina: Sierra de Guara II, 1:40,000
- Centro Geográfico del Ejército (CGDE) 249 Alquézar 30–11 (1:50,000)

Costa Blanca
- Michelin Costa Blanca road map (123 Zoom; 1:130,000)

- CGDE (not very reliable but the best available): 821 Alcoy 29-32; 822 Benisa 30-32; 846 Ibi 28-33; 847 Villajoyosa 29-33 (all 1:50,000)

Mallorca
- GeoCenter Mallorca road map (1:160,000)
- CGDE: 670 Soller 38-26; 671 Inca 39-26; 643/644 Pollença (38/39-25) (1:50,000)

23

Haute-Provence
- Michelin road map 245 (1:200,000)
- (for Apt) Institut Géographique National (IGN) maps: 31420T and 32420T
- (for Verdon) IGN map: 34420T

Sardinia
- Insight Travel road map (1:300,000)
- (for Badde Pentumas, Cala Gonone and Codola Fuili) Instituto Geografico Militar (IGM) map: 500 (Nuoro Est)
- (for Gorropu) IGM map: 517 (Baunei)

USING THIS GUIDE

This guide is broken down into three country sections – Spain, Italy and France – and, within these, into subsections covering the five canyoning areas – the Sierra de Guara, the Costa Blanca, Mallorca, Haute-Provence and Sardinia. The 'Practicalities' section in each subsection provides further information on transport, when to go, accommodation, maps, guides and other activities available in the area. Overview maps of each area are provided at the start of each section to help you locate the routes and get the hang of the topography. With the exception of Provence, the routes are grouped within quite a small area in each case.

Each area has a selection of canyons covering a spread of difficulties, so you can choose according to your level of experience or ambition. Routes are graded according to difficulty (see 'Route grading and quality', below). At the start of each route description, there is a summary giving: (in the title) quality (star rating), grade, water flow and (in the information box) length, descent, gear required, maps, season and timings for approach, descent and return.

Most of the canyon descriptions are accompanied by a sketch map, and in some cases a topo diagram is also included. The complex topography of the Guara and Verdon areas, where composite river systems feed into each other, results in a high concentration of canyons, and this is reflected in the layout of the sections. In the other areas the canyons are more isolated. In either case, a good road map will be an asset when it comes to locating the routes (see 'Maps and guides' in the 'Practicalities' section for recommendations for each area).

Appendix 1 provides a glossary of technical terms and geographical features. Appendix 6 is a full route summary table, with details of grade, quality, type of rock, length in kilometres, descent in metres, season, estimated time, gear required and cars needed for each route. You can also select your routes according to their difficulty, using the list in Appendix 5.

TECHNICAL ASPECTS OF CANYON DESCENT

To walk safely through the maze…
one needs the light of wisdom and the
guidance of virtue.

Buddha

ROUTE GRADING AND QUALITY

There are several different grading systems in use for canyons, and no single system is yet universally accepted. However, numerical systems going from 1 (easiest) to 5 or 6 (hardest) are commonly used, and a 1–6 system is used in this guide, with + or - to indicate variations. (See Appendix 5 for a full graded list of routes in ascending order of difficulty.) Note that grades are subjective and can only provide a rough estimate of difficulty and/or seriousness. For instance, a route of a given grade may be short and sharp, or technically easy but relatively long and committing. Also, a grade is given for a canyon under average conditions: when exceptionally heavy water is flowing any canyon will become much

ROUTE QUALITY

*	OK
**	good
***	better
****	brilliant

ROUTE GRADING – DIFFICULTY

Grade 1	easy hiking and wading
Grade 2	may involve long swimming sections or short abseils
Grade 3	more difficulty and commitment, eg tricky route-finding in boulder chokes, longer abseil pitches
Grade 4	longer canyons with many water passages, tricky scrambling and/or committing, long or awkward abseil pitches
Grade 5	as for Grade 4, only more so
Grade 6	as for Grade 5, but with serious sections such as floodable cave passages or long technical cave sections that may be hazardous in flood.
HS	a 'hard severe' rock climb, according to UK rock climbing gradings. (Only one route in this guide (Route 43) has a rock climbing pitch.)
≈	indicates that a route is significantly more difficult in heavy water flow and that heavy water flow is a distinct possibility.

harder (often impassable) and much more dangerous. A star system is used to indicate the route quality – reflecting scenery, situation, and sustained interest over the gorge's length.

SAFETY PRECAUTIONS

As you would if you were going walking, climbing or caving, it is a good idea to leave details of your chosen route with friends, or at the campsite, or in your tent or car. Plan to avoid long approaches in the heat of the day. Taking a mobile phone is a good idea but don't expect to pick up a signal in the canyon. Most canyons have inescapable sections, some several kilometres long. Check for possible escape routes (identified in this guide or others). Carry enough water. In dry periods you can't rely on there being potable water in the canyon – any water in the pools may be really rank!

Insurance and mountain rescue information is given in Appendix 3 and first aid basics in Appendix 4. Even more than you would on the hills at home, be aware of the dangers of having an accident or becoming stranded. Even a minor accident resulting in, for example, mild concussion or a sprained ankle, could put you in a much more serious situation in a canyon than it would on a hillside, crag or mountain ridge where a helicopter or stretcher team would have relatively easy access. So:

Steep rock walls in the lower Artuby (Route 40)

- don't jump into unknown pools
- abseil with caution
- strongly consider wearing a helmet in wet canyons.

It's fair to treat some canyons, such as the Mascún Inferior (Route 10), as fun-filled romps close to the comforts of civilisation. But some of the more remote canyons may only see a few canyoners a year and there will be no one on hand to help.

Be fit and confident enough for your chosen route. If you find that canyoning is too stressful for you to enjoy without help, hire a guide, or accept that it is not for you. (You can hire a guide easily in the Guara and Verdon areas and details are provided in the relevant sections.)

TEAM SIZE

The optimum size of your party depends on the nature of the canyon. On an easy, walking descent there is no real limit to the size the group can be – on a sunny summer's day in the Rio Vero (Route 1) dozens of groups happily meander downriver and there is a sense of safety in numbers. However, in other areas, and on more technical descents, your group is quite likely to be alone in your chosen canyon. This adds to the seriousness and it means that if you meet with an accident somebody may have to go it alone to get help. So, although a team of two is most efficient, a larger group of three or four offers more flexibility if things go wrong.

The major downside of a big group is that, on a route with abseil pitches, the larger your party the more time is spent hanging around waiting for all the members of your team to descend the rope. As well as causing frustrating delays for your own team, and for any teams behind, this may lead to cold, fatigue and even exposure if you are in cold water. On balance, two or three is probably the ideal number for speed in most canyons, but two teams of two, each fully equipped with rope, is ideal from the safety point of view (and will also give plenty of photo opportunities!).

Even the difficult canyons in this book are regularly done solo by confident canyoners. Although solo descents come with a serious health warning, they are perfectly feasible for the experienced and can be very satisfying adventures. In the end it's up to you to make a responsible decision on the size of your group based on your experience and the prevailing conditions.

EQUIPMENT AND CLOTHING

The exact gear you need for a descent depends factors such as the season, length of the canyon, whether it is wet or dry, and whether you will need to abseil. For each route, the gear you need is summarised in the route description and also in the route summary table in Appendix 6.

In the easiest Grade 1 canyons you are basically just walking; there may be some scrambling and wading, perhaps a bit of swimming thrown in for fun, but essentially your equipment needs are those of a walker. For Grade 2 and up, you will need extra kit over and above this basic level. Some of the Grade 2 canyons, and the majority of the canyons of Grade 3 or harder, require a rope, harness and abseil device. Those Grade 2s that don't require a rope, such as the Barrasil or Mascún Inferior (Routes 10 and 12), have long swimming stretches that you can't avoid. For most Grade 3s and up, you'll need both a rope and a wetsuit.

As ever in the outdoors, one person's luxury is another's essential, and there is much room for personal choice. What follows is a list of the minimum kit necessary for a descent according to the nature of your canyon.

Locking karabiners, a belay plate, krabs with slings, a lightweight waterproof (good for wearing under a one-piece wetsuit), sun cream and a dry bag

Canyoning gear, including harness, wetsuit and rope – a 10–15m rope is an asset for canyons with predominantly short abseils

Footwear

Whatever canyon you descend, walking will form a major part of your day. Wear sturdy trainers or lightweight boots with good grippy soles that you can wade or swim in, and that stay comfortable when they are full of water. Leather boots may be acceptable if they are light and can take a soaking, but wellington boots are a very bad idea.

Wetsuits and socks

For canyoning, perfectly adequate wetsuits needn't be expensive, and the sports superstore Decathlon (try www.decathlon.co.uk to find your local branch) is a good place to buy gear. If you are in Rodellar (Sierra de Guara) you can rent wetsuits at the campsites.

Whether you rent or buy, get a wetsuit that fits: too tight and it will be uncomfortable; too loose and it will be inefficient as an insulating layer. A 'shortie' (a one-piece suit, often with sleeves above the elbows and legs above the knees) or 'Farmer Johns' (the inner garment of a two-piece wetsuit, with full legs but a vest-like top) may suffice in summer, or in a canyon with short aquatic sections.

In the spring or autumn, or in a long, wet canyon, you will be much more comfortable in a full suit, which gives you two layers over your torso and the luxury of a hood with a zip that goes up to your chin. If you naturally feel the cold, opt for relatively thicker material and the extra insulation afforded by a full suit. Additionally, if you are not a strong swimmer, you will feel more comfortable with the added buoyancy. When abseiling down a waterfall (a feature of canyons of Grade 4 and above), the hood and extra buoyancy afforded by a full suit are major advantages. In easier, but very long, wet canyons (for example, the Peonara – Routes 13 and 14) you will spend a lot of time swimming, and as you lose a lot of heat through your head, a full suit is essential.

On hot days, a full suit presents you with the option of dispensing with your jacket, which can feel heavy and cumbersome. On marginal days where you're unsure whether to take the full suit, a lightweight waterproof under your farmer Johns is a good compromise. Waterproof mountain-biking socks are good for keeping your feet warm in long aquatic canyons, and are much better than neoprene bootees for wearing inside lightweight boots or trainers.

Rucksack, dry bag and general kit

If you habitually carry the kitchen sink in a big rucksack, think again. It will slow you down and drive you mad getting stuck in narrows. It will also increase the risk of you slipping on a wet rock, losing your balance or spraining your ankle. A small daysack is much better. Carry a whistle and a pocket knife, and maybe a torch if you plan on – or might risk – being out

late. On the walk-in, it's often easier to carry your wetsuit over your shoulder or tied to your back with a rope than it is to try and stuff it in a small sack.

A dry bag or a hard plastic waterproof container is a must for storing cameras, first aid, maps, guides, valuables and lunch. Buy one before you leave home if you can, as they are not always available locally. Dry bags look like stuff sacs, but are waterproof and sealable by means of a stiff rim that folds over several times before clipping into itself. They work well but you may experience some angst depending on the value of your camera! If you opt for a hard plastic container, it should be small enough to fit in your pack with room to spare, so you don't have to open it every time you want to stow something.

Finally, consider wearing a helmet – wet boulders can be extemely slippery.

When you're in the canyon, tie up any superfluous dangling rucksack straps – or risk embarrassment as you hang helplessly when they snag on a simple bum-slide.

Rope, abseil device, harness and related gear

Many Grade 1 and 2 canyons require no abseiling or expertise with ropes. However, possession of a harness, a rope or two, some slings, karabiners and a belay/abseil device opens up many more possibilities. A single rope of 40 or 50m is all you need for most

Smooth slabs require a swarm rope in the Golade Gorropu (Route 43)

of the canyons in this book, although some require two 50m ropes. A shorter rope of 10–20m is also a handy asset, as it doesn't take long to get thoroughly fed up with coiling and uncoiling an unnecessarily long rope.

Ropes can be either dynamic or static. All climbing ropes are of the dynamic variety – designed to stretch, enabling them to absorb shock loads and confer less force on a belay system or a falling climber. Broadly speaking, climbing ropes are available in 9mm, 10mm and 11mm diameters and lengths of 45–60m. The best choice for canyoning is a 9mm rope, as it is light and allows free-running abseils with almost any belay plate.

Climbing ropes can of course be used for abseiling, and most climbers will be happy to use a normal leading rope, or preferably a 'retired' leading rope that might have taken a few falls but can still be used safely for abseiling. Static or semi-static ropes are equally good for abseiling, but are better for ascending as they don't stretch or bounce so much under load (they must not be used for lead climbing, or in any situation where stretch is vital). Static rope, normally cheaper than dynamic rope, can be bought by the metre and is generally available in 9, 10, 10.5, 11 or 11.5mm x 50, 100, 150 or 200m (10.5mm x 50m is the most popular combination). If you are buying a rope specifically for canyoning,

31

Clipping a belay/abseil anchor (Route 41)

it's probably best to choose a static rope; but be aware of its limitations.

On all the routes in this book where you need a rope, you also need a harness, several slings and karabiners (screwgates and snapgates) for clipping in to fixed gear on abseil stations, and an abseil device. This forms the basic set of gear you will need for getting yourself down any pitch.

Harness

Any climbing sit-harness, whether it's designed for sport-climbing or mountaineering, is good for canyoning. A caving harness or a full-body mountaineering harness will also serve the purpose. Whatever harness you use, though, be aware that a few bumslides over rough rock can knock hell out of your leg-loops and may weaken them substantially.

Slings and karabiners

A couple of long slings forming a cow's tail or lanyard are required for clipping in to *in situ* ropes or cables on traverse sections. These should be used in conjunction with screw-gate krabs on belays. On cable traverses, snap-gates are easier to handle and are safe enough, especially if you always have multiple slings clipped in and keep them under tension.

Rope and belay technique

It goes without saying that you need to be able to use this equipment. As a bare minimum, you will need to know how to clip in to an anchor and make

yourself safe, and be able to abseil confidently (that is, without needing a safety rope). In addition, members of the team should be able to belay someone on a traverse, to ascend a rope, to lower an injured person and other basic rescue ropework. Carry (and know how to use) Prusik or a Shunt for safeguarding abseils and these or other devices for ascending a rope.

Abseil devices

It's assumed that you will have learned how to abseil safely before you go canyoning. That said, it will be well worth reading this section if you haven't abseiled in a while.

Use the abseil device you are most comfortable with for the rope you are using – be it a modern belay plate, figure-8, Sticht plate, Reverso or whatever. The device you use will probably depend on whether you're a climber, caver or just someone who abseils occasionally.

If you're an 'occasional abseiler' and no more, the chances are that you happily use a figure-8. However, figure-8s are heavy and cause the rope to twist. Moreover, recent evidence might have you worried: figure-8s can, in certain situations, twist against the gate of a screwgate karabiner and break it open. If you use a figure-8, get a specialised karabiner to counteract this, such as a DMM Belay Master.

Most climbers these days don't carry a figure-8 for abseiling, preferring to use their belay plate. Most belay plates can safely be used for abseiling in most situations, although they heat up more quickly than a large figure-8. If you're a climber buying a new belay plate that you also want to use for canyoning, or you have a few different devices on your climbing rack, choose one with two wide slots. Don't necessarily go for those recommended as 'safest' – those with the most friction. Although these are perfectly good for belaying, many are quite tight on an 11mm rope, and all the abseiling you do when canyoning will be on double ropes, with all the extra friction that implies. It is better to choose a device that suits the diameter of your rope.

If you're a caver, you probably won't need much advice from this book on how to abseil, but you may want to reassess the suitability of your kit. In a canyon, your gear needs to be suitable for abseiling on double ropes. You need to pull your ropes down after each pitch, and carry them down the canyon. So the single rope technique kit won't be much use, and if you carry a 100m static line you'll feel more like a beast of burden than a happy canyoner.

Whatever method you choose, get to know how your gear performs on short, slabby pitches before you launch into a free 50m abseil

down an overhang. Although the use of a Prusik loop or a Shunt to safeguard yourself while descending is highly recommended in most abseiling situations, **this is not usually the case when abseiling into water or down a waterfall because of a risk of drowning** (see 'Special Considerations in Aquatic Canyons', below).

Fixed gear

Aiding across a fixed traverse line – note the additional safety rope

Bolts on a traverse: with a few krabs, these can be temporarily rigged with a safety line if a fixed rope isn't already in position

The importance of solid, 100 per cent reliable anchors cannot be over-stressed. Make sure that your anchors are the best available, and whenever possible use an abseil station with multiple anchor points. Always avoid abseiling off a single anchor. Belay anchors are usually impossible not to leave behind as you descend the canyon and pull your ropes. Therefore, barring enterprising theft by maraud-ing helicopter crews, they will invari-ably be *in situ*. Most will be double bolts. In case you can't find them or they are badly corroded, take some spare disposable abseil slings or rope.

SOME TECHNIQUES

The technical aspects of canyoning have something in common with caving, including the presence of bolted abseil stations and the occa-sional boulder choke, and the water-worn passages in some canyons resemble the easy passages in Yorkshire's Long Churn Pot or Dow Cave, or Swildon's Hole in the Mendips. Sometimes the route-find-ing can also be very three-dimen-sional, but there the resemblance with caving ends. A sun-drenched Spanish canyon is about as far as you could possibly imagine from crawl-ing around in a dark muddy hole in the UK on a cold winter's day.

Route-finding

On any descent, good route-finding skills are a great asset. In an easy, wide canyon, there may be several possible routes, and your team will split up, find its own way through, reunite and repeat the process almost like the water in the stream itself. However, in constricted or steep canyons, boulder chokes can be quite challenging, and some patience is often required to find the easiest route through the maze. Stay three-dimensionally aware and be prepared to backtrack if things look tricky, rather than attempt something that seems unreasonably hazardous. There will almost certainly be an easy way down if you hunt around. Often it's best for the less experienced to hang back while a leader makes small reconnaissance trips, returning to help the others through the maze, rather than have everyone moving together at once.

Abseiling

In the canyons described in this vol-ume, the huge majority of abseil sta-tions are well maintained and two-bolt stainless steel anchors are stan-dard – but not all. It pays to carry some spare cord or tape so that you can back up any suspect anchors. Abseil slings should be treated with caution, as the UV in direct sunlight is damaging even over short periods. Ideally a metal link or Maillon should be in place to eliminate friction between the rope and the sling. Tape or sling anchors should be equalised so that a central point bears the load-ing, but this is not always what you find in practice. Be prepared to cut

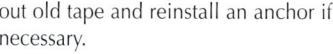

Plant your feet well apart, lean back, go slow…easy!

Using side walls and tension for balance

out old tape and reinstall an anchor if necessary.

The following advice is intended to prevent abseiling accidents. It applies to descents with a descender such as a figure-8, or with a Sticht plate or other belay plate (which you are not supposed to use for abseiling, even though all climbers do). Cavers, who may prefer to use specialised descenders, will doubtless use their established methods.

Set up the abseil to allow the rope to run through smoothly. Think ahead. What's the best way to thread the anchor? What will happen when you pull the rope from below – will it run smoothly or snag?

The equipment

Different belay plates and abseil devices provide different levels of friction, with relatively new or thin ropes providing less resistance than thick or older ropes: make sure you know what to expect from the combination you use. In particular take care when using a figure-8 to abseil because it can misalign itself across the karabiner gate. If it becomes even lightly loaded when misaligned it can lever open and detach itself from a properly screwed up karabiner with dire consequences. Serious injuries and deaths have resulted from this.

A single bolt anchor – not ideal

Old bolts, old tat – look around for something better

Abseiling – part of the fun or an evil necessity?

For many, abseiling is an activity to be avoided. It is spurned as a needlessly hazardous activity by many climbers, unless it is the only way of getting off a climb or down a mountain. It has claimed many lives over the years, including those of the great Scottish mountaineer Tom Patey and, recently, the American climber Todd Skinner in Yosemite. In the words of the British Mountaineering Council's website:

'A common and false perception of abseiling is that it is an adventure activity that is completely safe. But as many have discovered accidents do occur even in controlled circumstances…abseil ropes cut through, failed anchors, detached karabiners, and abseil devices that "mysteriously" did not control the speed of descent. Add to this clothing and long hair tangled in the abseil device; trips, flips and swings; the end of a rope being reached unexpectedly; plus the odd jammed rope, sharp edge and falling rock or piece of a equipment, and you have a much clearer understanding of the hazards of abseiling and why it claims lives. As with all methods of descending abseiling is dangerous; but it is particularly unforgiving of any mistakes or failures.'

It's worth noting that Skinner's death was caused by the failure of his harness belay loop, an event almost unimaginable to most climbers, who would regard it as the safest link in the belay chain. Skinner's unfortunate accident underlines the fact that, when abseiling, your life depends completely on the state of your gear and the way you use it. Therefore, **check your kit regularly and retire anything old or worn.**

Rockfall and sharp edges

When setting up the abseil avoid positions with loose rock or sharp edges in the area where the rope will run. If it is unavoidable to abseil down loose material, remove the worst of it to pre-empt pulling it down when the rope is retrieved. A loaded rope stretched over a sharp edge can be severed with surprising ease: if there is no alternative, use some form of rope protector.

When you start to abseil, be careful not to kick rocks onto those below, or dislodge material above you by swinging sideways. Keep an eye on the karabiner gate to ensure that it has not accidentally opened. Ensure long hair, straps or clothing don't get caught.

Abseil smoothly and directly down the fall line and avoid bounces or pendulums that may draw the rope across an edge. Use of a friction karabiner between a belay plate and your locking karabiner can give extra control, but can result in over-fast descent on a thin rope and might be fiddly to keep hold of and even dangerous in water (best to unclip it before touchdown): use your experience.

Note that typically the breaking load for a karabiner long axis is about 22kN, compared with only 6kN across the gate, which could be exceeded in a shock loading situation. Separate knots in each end of the rope are sensible precautions on a long abseil, but don't forget to untie them before trying to retrieve the rope. Always **consider** using a Prusik or other back-up system on the abseil rope in case you need to rest, sort out a tangle or guard against losing control. **But do not use such a device when abseiling into a pool under a waterfall, where you may drown if you can't detach from the rope quickly**. (See 'Special Considerations in Aquatic Canyons, below.)

THE ABSEIL

Before starting to abseil:
- Stay clipped into the anchor until you have checked everything and are ready to go.
- Check that both ends of the rope reach the bottom.
- If you have two ropes tied together, remember which one to pull.
- Check the rope will pull smoothly and is not over any sharp edges.
- Check that your karabiner is screwed closed and that it will become loaded end-to-end rather than across the gate.
- Lower your weight gently onto the karabiner/abseil device, rather than with a sudden movement that may shock-load it.
- Weight the rope with a short 'mini-abseil' of a few centimetres before unclipping the anchor.

Entering the Mascún Sup – a committing manoeuvre right at the start of the gorge (Route 7)

AT AN INTERMEDIATE ANCHOR

- Clip in with a short cow's tail or two.
- Tie off a slack loop in rope, or thread one end (the end you intend to pull) through the anchor and tie it off or hang on to it.
- Make space for the rest of the team.

AT THE BOTTOM

When you get to the bottom of the pitch:

- Give the rope a test pull to see whether it's running smoothly for retrieval.
- Get your partner to rectify any problems up top.
- Don't wander off just yet...instead, safeguard subsequent descents from below by holding onto the rope ready to pull it tight in the event of an uncontrolled descent.
- When everybody is down, pull the rope firmly and smoothly.
- In murky or deep water, hang on to the rope until you can coil or bag it at a convenient spot.

Hold your nose – fun rapids in the Peonara Šup (Route 13)

Jammed rope

Fortunately, a rope becoming stuck is relatively unlikely in a canyon, as the anchors are usually well planned and the water-washed rock is smooth. Try to plan ahead and prevent jams: if the rope snags around a spike or tree as it falls, you can encounter serious delay or danger. Try to flick and tug from different angles to free it. If you still have both ends of the rope you will be able to either Prusik up, or climb up while tying in at intervals to protect yourself.

If the rope has only partly pulled through leaving you with just one end, consider whether you can use another rope, or part of the stuck rope, to lead up. If there is no way you can climb back up, consider cutting the rope and continuing. Do not Prusik on a single rope as it could pull free at any moment with fatal consequences. Only ascend a stuck rope as a very last resort – it's very scary and extremely dangerous.

Joining two ropes

A 50m rope is adequate for abseiling almost all of the canyons in this book, but for a longer abseil where it is necessary to join two ropes:

- one of the most reliable knots is a double fisherman's with tails at least eight to ten times the rope diameter. The downsides are that it's hard to undo once loaded and it tends to get stuck on projections rather than rolling off them;
- the double figure-8 is just as reliable and easier to undo than the double fisherman's but it is perhaps even more likely to get stuck when pulling the ropes;
- the single figure-8, with long tails, is widely used; however, it can roll and is increasingly regarded as dangerous, especially with wet ropes and/or when badly tied;
- the overhand knot (see below), also with long tails, can also

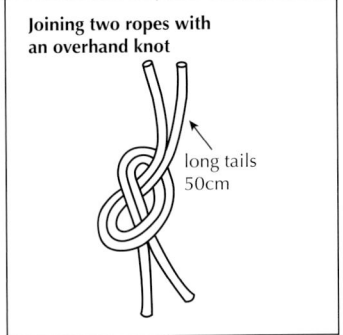

Joining two ropes with an overhand knot

long tails 50cm

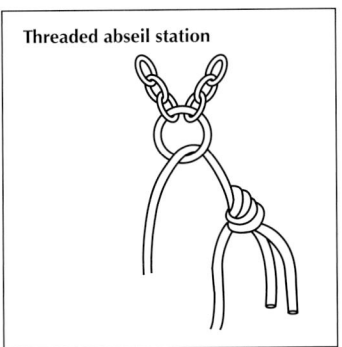

Threaded abseil station

invert but is less likely to than the single figure-8 – therefore it is the **recommended** knot.

- another option is to use two adjacent overhand knots. This removes the inverting problem seen with the single figure-8 or overhand knots (thanks to Stephen Reid on www.needlesports.com).

Debate continues about the best way to join ropes. (The evidence is discussed at www.needlesports.com.)

To pass a knot that joins ropes in mid-pitch, the normal procedure is to tie a loop knot in the end of the upper rope below the knot used to join the ropes. A cow's tail attached to this loop allows abseil checks to be carried out with more slack than when just using an ascender above the knot.

Teamwork
Multi-pitch abseils or long series of abseils are time-consuming. An efficient team will work together, with one retrieving the rope while the other feeds the free end through the next anchor.

Finding the anchors
If you can't find an anchor when you need it, ask yourself whether it's on the other side of the canyon, hidden behind a tree or a boulder, or have you passed it already. On very long multi-pitch abseils it is possible to miss out a belay station, only to find

Sierra de Guara landscape

The hike to the Oscuros de Balcés takes in some amazing wilderness scenery (Route 15)

ABSEILING SUMMARY

- Back up your anchors if necessary.
- Keep yourself and your ropes attached to anchor points.
- Abseil smoothly.
- Keep the rope clear of loose rock and sharp edges.
- Take precautions to avoid losing control or abseiling off the ends of the rope.
- Do a test pull after the first canyoner completes the abseil.
- Don't use a Prusik or Shunt if abseiling into a waterfall pool.

---

the rope running out in the middle of nowhere: go slow!

Other situations requiring ropes

In a canyon, there may be short sections of fixed rope, usually knotted, that can be descended or ascended hand-over-hand. More often than not these ropes are old, worn and frayed. Always check for abrasions and wear and, if in doubt, abseil. A touch of rock-climbing technique and arm strength is needed to descend fixed rope hand-over-hand, even if the knots are nice and chunky. This is especially true if the rock is steep, wet or slimy. Again, if in doubt, consider abseiling.

On traverses, there may be fixed cables that you can clip in to. Normally you would use your cow's tails, but, if the cable is missing or damaged, you may need to lead the pitch as you would on a rock-climb, clipping runners into the fixed gear as you go.

Unless confronted by an abseil pitch, canyoners, like hill walkers and climbers, shouldn't really have to resort to using the rope. It's almost always quicker and safer to explore

other descent options. However, in greasy conditions some standard descents can become awkward and perhaps dangerous. A short abseil, or perhaps lowering over a short drop, is sensible in these conditions.

SPECIAL CONSIDERATIONS IN AQUATIC CANYONS

The force of flowing water generates some of the major hazards in canyoning. It is often a new experience for many new canyoners coming from a mountain-activity background (although surfers may find it easy to adjust). The only comparable scenario is crossing a swollen stream following a wet day on the hill. The power of flowing water demands respect. It makes sense not to rush straight for the hardest canyons but to build your experience gradually. The following points are the minimum you should consider. Get hold of one of the many instruction manuals that exist in Spanish or French for more definitive coverage. The major hazards are summarised in the diagram (right).

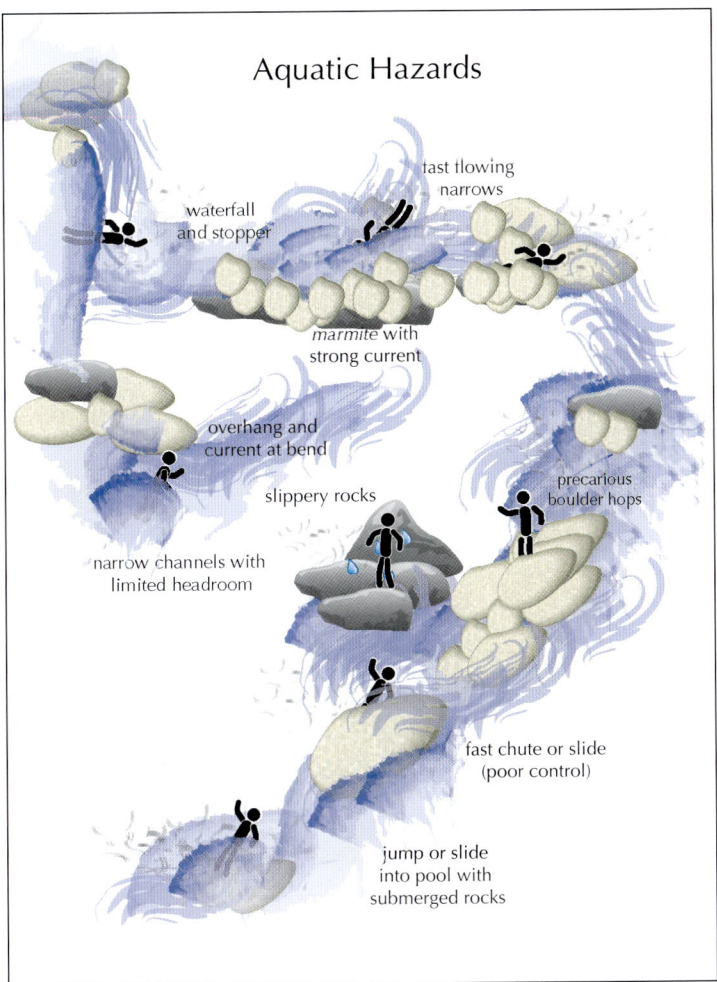

Aquatic Hazards

waterfall and stopper

fast flowing narrows

marmite with strong current

overhang and current at bend

precarious boulder hops

slippery rocks

narrow channels with limited headroom

fast chute or slide (poor control)

jump or slide into pool with submerged rocks

The force of flowing water is almost always stronger than you are. It can flip you around or over with ease, and an innocuous-looking waterslide might send you spinning out of control. Mind your head – a helmet is advisable.

45

Look out for currents and siphons. Currents can sweep you under boulders, under overhangs or into submerged caves. Be very wary of this happening, especially in heavy water flow, as you can get pinned under the surface. Look out for the members of your group – especially the younger, smaller and lighter ones. Keep a special eye out for rolling sumps and siphons. If someone is sucked down a siphon and disappears, they obviously need help fast, but don't go directly after them except as a very last resort. Avoid the force of downward-flowing water at all costs, or you're likely to join them. Get downstream and come towards the hazard from below, or from one side. Proceed speedily but cautiously.

Upstream hydroelectric activity – beware of sudden releases of masses of water

Abseiling in a waterfall is a risky manoeuvre. Sounds easy, right? In fact the major cause of fatal accidents in canyoning is drowning while abseiling, resulting from a failure to detach from the rope. This isn't a problem in the easier, wider canyons, as the pools are shallow and the abseil points are placed so as to keep you out of the waterfalls. However, in a narrow canyon there may be no alternative but to abseil down the line of a waterfall into a deep pool. The force of a waterfall can push you under the surface with astonishing ease, and unless you get off the rope you can get stuck. Don't even think about doing this without a wetsuit – the buoyancy it confers is crucial, and you need to keep your hands free for ropework rather than swimming. Needless to say, check that there are no snags in the rope and that it runs free. Avoid using an 11mm rope and belay plate – you need to be able to unclip quickly and easily. A 9mm rope and/or a tube-style belay device or a figure-8 is better. **It can't be overstressed that you should not use Prusiks or a Shunt in this situation** – your aim should be to get off the rope as soon as you hit the water.

A short rope can be handy. You don't really want to carry more rope than you need, and apart from the hassle of coiling and uncoiling a long rope, in water it can be safer to customise its length. If you have an old rope, cut it to size – advice on pitch lengths is given in all the route chapters. If

you're *rapping* into a fast flowing channel, a technique that works well is to keep paying out the rope so that you float downstream (this worked well for me on the third pitch of the Oscuros de Balcés (Route 15), where I was having trouble fighting my urge to climb freehand back up the rope to extricate myself from the raging torrent falling on my head!). Again, getting off the rope is the objective; abseiling off the ends while afloat is one way of doing it.

Water flow is a major variable. Some canyons can be made much more difficult in, or following, wet periods. The symbol ≈ is used in the text for those canyons most affected. Keep an eye on the weather, and size up the likely water flow in your canyon. Bear the following questions in mind. How much has it rained recently? Is there a daily rainfall pattern, for example afternoon storms (these can be violent and sudden, and are common in summer and autumn)? What's the weather forecast? Is there a dam or hydroelectric scheme upstream that regulates water flow (if you're in the Verdon, the answer is Yes, and sudden changes are common). Be prepared to change your plans and walk out.

Don't get snagged or stuck. Don't hang slings (or too many krabs) from

47

Looking down to L'Artuby's aquatic narrows (Route 40)

your body or harness – they can get snagged on rocks or logs when you're swimming or sliding. Keep them in your sac or tucked in your wetsuit.

Don't jump into pools without first checking what's in them or how deep they are.

Step carefully. A simple slip from a wet boulder may result in a grisly fall or a headlong dive into a foaming stopper.

Don't lose your rope. This may sound stupid, but it happens. Ropes sink in water. Knots can easily work loose when you're swimming and sliding. I once lost a rope that was tied around my waist and shoulders, in murky, violent water, fortunately after the last abseil pitch of the day. Use a back-up knot, or invest in a canyoning rope bag and stow the rope after each abseil.

SPAIN

Although Spain is a large, mountainous country studded with impressive limestone massifs, 20 years ago its climbing and walking was obscure by European
standards. Now, Spanish climbing is world-famous and Spain's canyons fully
deserve to be recognised as some of the best around. The canyons of the Sierra de
Guara rule the roost, and, along with those of the rugged semi-coastal coastal
ranges of Mallorca and the Costa Blanca, make Spain the sun-canyoning capital
of the Mediterranean.

SIERRA DE GUARA

The canyons of the Sierra de Guara lie in the pre-Pyrenees, to the south of the
main mountain chain in the province of Huesca. They are widely known amongst
Spanish and French canyoning enthusiasts as one of the finest collections in the
Pyrenean area – and in my view the Guara canyons are the best, the right stuff,
those by which all others must be judged.

Dozens of gorges? Unclimbed rock? ...come to the Sierra de Guara

Approaches to the Sierra de Guara

The tiny village of Rodellar, perched above the cliffs of the Rio Mascún, at 761m, has been a major centre for canyoning since the 1980s. Surprisingly, Rodellar has changed little during the last 10 years or so, and the influx of summer holidaymakers has not, so far, led to the invasive tourist development that has affected places like Gavarnie across the border in France. The landscape is an uncompromising limestone upland massif, where rocky gorges cut deep between pointed peaks in a wasteland of Mediterranean scrub. The deep ravines exemplify all things Spanish and mysterious that 'descenso de canyones' has to offer. The selection listed here is by no means exhaustive (there are well over 70 documented descents in the Sierra de Guara alone), but all of these canyons are very worthwhile. The easier ones can be done in a few hours, while the longer ones are more serious and will take a fit team most of a full day.

Practicalities

Getting there

There are dozens of flights to Barcelona taking off every day from most UK airports. Budget airlines operating to Barcelona include EasyJet from Bristol, Liverpool, Newcastle, Gatwick, Stansted, and Luton; Ryanair from Blackpool, Bournemouth, Dublin, Glasgow, Liverpool, Nottingham, Stansted and Luton; Jet2 from Belfast and Leeds to Barcelona; Globespan from Edinburgh and Glasgow; ThomsonFly from Coventry, Glasgow, Gatwick, Manchester and Newcastle; and Monarch from Manchester. British Airways has several daily flights from Gatwick and Heathrow, and several scheduled flights a week from Birmingham. Iberia Airlines has scheduled daily flights from Heathrow and Dublin. Aer Lingus (www.aerlingus.com) serves Barcelona from Cork and Dublin. Approach by rail is feasible as far as Huesca, which is served by a branch line from Zaragoza.

The Sierra, with a high point of 2077m, lies about 40km south of the main Pyrenean watershed, to the north-east of the Aragonese town of Huesca, which in turn is 70km north-east of Zaragoza. From Barcelona the drive takes about 3h. Head east to Lleida and take the N240 to Barbastro. Continue towards Huesca, but take the turning north to Abiego, Bierge and Rodellar. If you are coming from Toulouse (about 4–5hrs), head over the Pyrenees to join the route at Barbastro.

As you approach the village of Rodellar, the road tantalisingly gains the crest of a ridge that marks the watershed between two major gorges, the Alcanadre and the Isuala, each with dramatic high cliffs and many side-canyons. Both gorges change in character many times over their length, never more emphatically so than when the sweeping, bright limestone gives way to the earthy-brown conglomerate that forms its bedrock.

When to go

Canyoning is possible all year round. Many of the canyons are at their best in the early summer when the copious flow of meltwater adds interest. July and August are good, but the canyons can be can be busy (especially in August), and approach walks can be arduous in the heat. September is pleasant and quiet, with few canyoners except at weekends, although conditions can be on the dry side. There will not be much in the way of campsite, shop or wetsuit hire facilities from October through to April or even May.

Where to stay

In the Sierra de Guara the most convenient place to camp is in Rodellar, where Camping Mascún (tel: (+34) 974 318367) has full facilities, a bar/restaurant and a shop. The campsite shop is well stocked with food, wine, maps, guides and full wetsuits for hire at very reasonable rates (5 or 6 Euros per jacket or shortie in

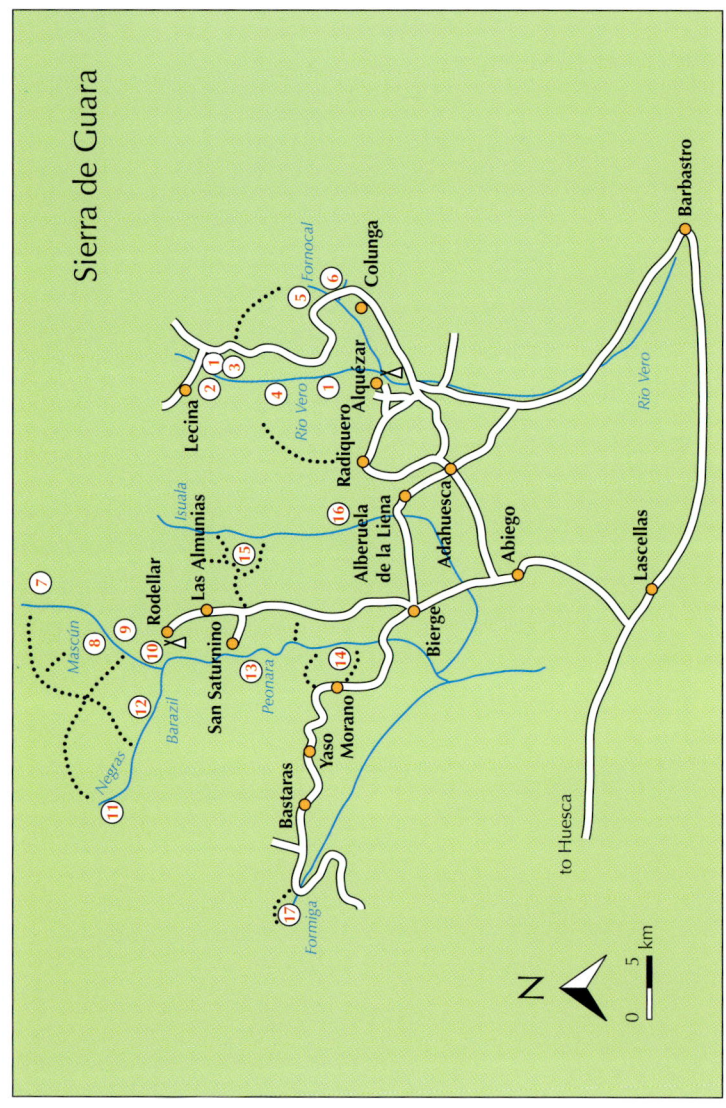

September 2004). Camping El Puente (tel: (+34) 974 318312) is 2km from Rodellar in the Alcanadre river valley. Camping Expeditiones (tel: (+34) 974 318336) is in the woods 6km south of Rodellar, near the village of Las Almunias, and there are *pensiones* and/or hostels in both Rodellar and Las Almunias. There is also camping at Lecina and more salubrious accommodation in Alquézar and Huesca.

Maps and guides

The Michelin road map 443 is good for getting you to the Guara area. Guara Sierra and Canyons Park (1:40,000, published by Pireneo in Huesca, 1998) and the official Spanish sheet 249 Alquézar 30–11 cover the Vero area. Several current guides to canyoning are in print in Spanish, French and German. Guides tend to go out of print or become superseded, but the topo-map 'Barranquismo en el Pirineo – Sierra de Guara' (P Gimet and J-P Pontroué; ISBN 2-9503199-5-5) is useful for an overview of the entire area. It is a very rough map but has information on the back (in English) that will get you to many canyons not featured in this guide, with grades, times and gear requirements. Canyoning, climbing and walking guides are generally available in the campsite shop and the village bar and guiding services are offered by the campsites.

Getting around

A car is useful but not essential if you can get to Rodellar by other means. In fact, one of the attractions of Rodellar as a canyoning base is the number of canyons you can walk to: of the routes listed here, four begin and end in the village and a

First water – a typical high-plateau start to a Guara canyon

further two finish at the Puente de Pedruel, only 2km away by road. For the further-flung canyons, hitchhiking is a possibility, especially as there is a culture in the area of fellow canyoners helping each other out. However, for easy access to the Rio Vero canyons and Formiga, you really need a vehicle.

Other activities

Many well-marked walking trails exist in the Rodellar area. Signposts by the church give details of some routes. A good circular route, taking in some spectacular scenery, is to descend into the Mascún gorge and head for the village of Otín (1074m). Walk upstream for 1km to the tributary canyon on the left and up this to the col (from here you can reach the Barrasil by descending the other side). Turn right (north) and continue gaining altitude. Once on the plateau, pass the dolmen of Losa Mora and continue north to Otín. Return by heading south-east, passing the Barranco de Otín and descending once again into the Mascún (4–5h).

The Mascún Gorge is peppered with crags of all description, from riverside slabs to huge tufa-encrusted caves, and is becoming a well-known venue for rock-climbing. As the Mascún runs north-to-south, finding shaded cliffs is possible at

Sierra de Guara Routes	Grade	Quality	Rock	Length (km)	Desc (m
1. Rio Vero	2+ 〰	****	L	8.0	20
2. Barranco de Basender	3	**	L	0.6	11
3. Barranco de Portiacha	4-	**	L	0.25	12
4. Barranco de Chimiachas	4	***	L	1.5	28
5. Barranco de Fornocal	3 〰	***	L/C	3.0	15
6. Barranco de las Palomeras	3 〰	**	C	0.35	7
7. Barranco de Mascún Superior	4+ 〰	****	L	2.5	14
8. Barranco de Otín	4+	***	L	0.5	24
9. Barranco de Mascún Inferior	1	**	L	3.5	5
10. Barranco de Mascún Inferior – last section	2 〰	*	L	1.7	3
11. Gorgas Negras	4 〰	***	L	4.5	15
12. Garganta de Barrasil	2+ 〰	**	L	2.5	6
13. Garganta de la Peonara Superior	2+	***	L	4.5	10
14. Garganta de la Peonara Inferior	3 〰	***	L	2.5	6
15. Oscuros de Balcés	4 〰	****	L	1.5	5
16. Estrechos de Balcés	2	*	C	6.5	10
17. Rio Formiga – Barranco de Yara	3 〰	**	C	1.5	6
C – conglomerate, L – limestone					

any time of day. Most pitches are fully bolted sport-climbs. There are about 200 routes in the Mascún Inferior, where easy access has concentrated developments, and quality multi-pitch climbs beckon from slightly more distant cliffs and pinnacles. Details of the climbing can be found in local guidebooks.

If it's raining, or you've had enough of canyoning, try a beer in the picturesque fortified hilltop village of Alquézar – but be prepared for tourist hordes in high season. If cave paintings are your thing, the ones spectacularly situated high on the eastern rim of the Rio Vero gorge are worth a visit – follow the signs from the Adahuesca–Arcusa road (A2205). Take some binoculars and watch the amazing gliding feats of the vultures (instead of them sizing you up, for a change).

Developed canyons are plentiful elsewhere in the Sierra de Guara, and also on the limestone massif of Monte Perdido further north. Over the border in France, the areas around Sainte Engrâce and Laruns (south of Pau) are canyoning centres (mostly grade 4 and up). If you're moving on or need a change of scene, the spectacular Mallos de Riglos and the Ordesa Gorge are within a few hours' drive.

Season	Time	Gear (optional/seasonal)		Access
pr–Oct	5hr30–6hr30 (one way)			2 cars or hitch/taxi from Alquézar
ll year	2hr40	rope		car
ll year	2hr30	rope		car
ll year	6hr30–7hr30	rope		car
ar–Oct	5hr40	rope, wetsuit		car
ll year	2hr40	rope, wetsuit		car
ay–Nov	7hr30–9hr	rope, wetsuit		walk from Rodellar
ll year	6hr30	rope (wetsuit)		walk from Rodellar
ar–Oct	5hr15	(wetsuit)		walk from Rodellar
ar–Oct	3hr15	wetsuit		walk from Rodellar
n–Oct	8hr–10hr	rope, wetsuit		walk from Rodellar
ay–Nov	4hr30–5hr30	wetsuit		walk from Rodellar
ay–Oct	5hr30	wetsuit		1–2 cars
ay–Nov	5hr	wetsuit		car
ay–Nov	4hr30	rope, wetsuit		car
ay–Nov	5hr30	wetsuit		2 cars
ay–Nov	3hr15	rope, wetsuit		car

THE ROUTES
Rio Vero area

Oh you who are born of the blood of the gods, Trojan son of Anchises, easy is the descent to Hell; the door of dark Dis stands open day and night. But to retrace your steps and come out to the air above, that is work, that is labour!

Virgil, The Aeneid

The massive canyon of the Vero will appeal to all lovers of wilderness grandeur and provides a great introduction to canyoning. Its more technical side-canyons are also well worth exploring, making this one of the finest canyoning areas in Spain.

1. Rio Vero **** 2+ 〰

Rock	limestone
Length	8km
Descent	200m
Gear	in the high season, T-shirt, shorts and trainers are adequate. Consider a wetsuit outside the hottest months, and a short rope (20m) for those lacking confidence or experience.
Season	April to October
Time	approach 5min, descent 5–6h, return 40min plus 20km by road
Maps	Editorial Alpina: Sierra de Guara II, 1:40,000 Centro Geográfico del Ejército (CGDE): 249 Alquézar 30–11, 1:50,000

A very popular expedition that requires no special skills or equipment, this is a long, easy ramble along the deepest and most spectacular gorge in the Sierra de Guara. With plenty of swimming sections and a lot of hiking and wading, the Vero is great fun. The torrents and boulder sections can be

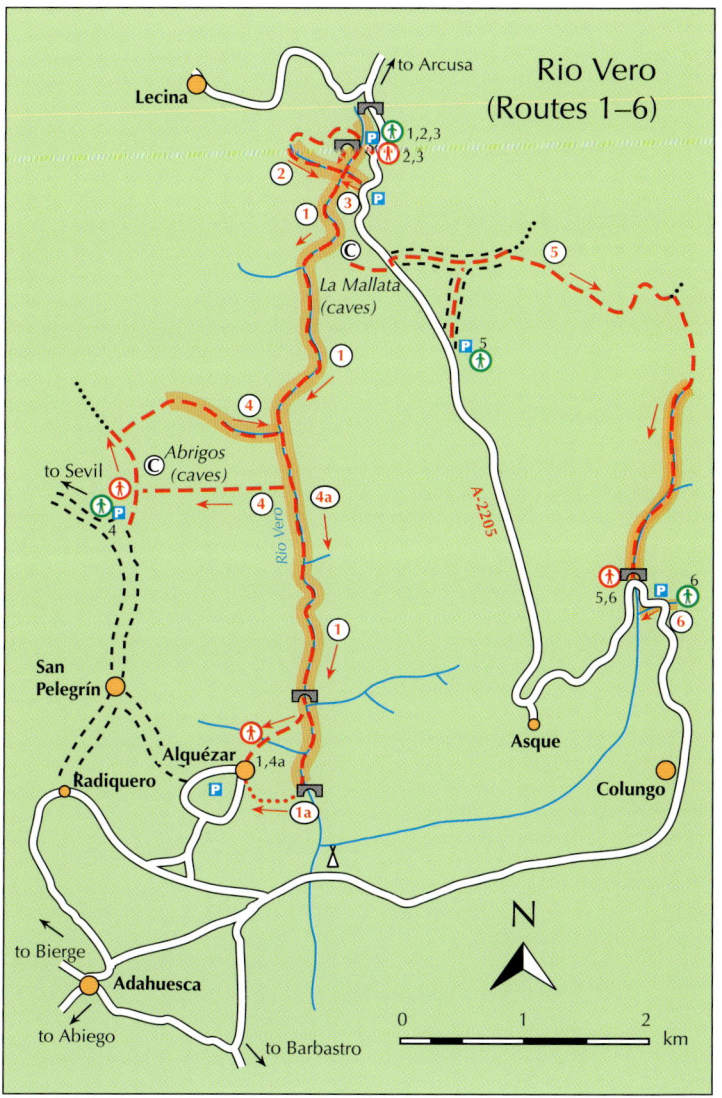

Rio Vero
(Routes 1–6)

57

negotiated directly for maximum excitement, or bypassed completely as desired. The steep cliffs either side of the gorge are dotted with cave chambers that once hosted prehistoric man and are now home to countless huge vultures. Eminently suitable for beginners and families, and very popular – don't expect solitude!

Access point:
about 20km from
Adahuesca

Approach

Ideally two cars are needed so that one can be left in Alquézar. Use the other to access the gorge entrance near Lecina: from Alquézar drive south to meet the Adahuesca–Arcusa road (A2205). Head east past the Camping Rio Vero, passing through the village of Colungo. Now in conglomerate country, pass over several canyons including the Barranco de las Palomeras (Route 6). Follow the road over the plateau. If time permits, it's worth taking a detour to the cliff-top cave dwellings at La Mallata (signposted, spectacular views, allow 1hr). A parking area is reached about 1km before a campsite and a road junction (left to Lecina left, right to Arcusa), above a bridge over the Vero. Hitchhiking is a feasible alternative.

Easy going in the Rio Vero's initial walking section

Descent

Walk down into the initial section of the gorge by the bridge, and continue along it crossing the river as necessary. Purists will try to stick to the watercourse. After 2km, a jump is followed by a swimming section. Other aquatic sections follow, including several atmospheric labyrinths and water-carved boulder chokes. After 8km, next to a bridge (Puente de Villacantal), a path to Alquézar leads up the hillside on the right. Alternatively, a **short extension** (Route 1a) can be made by following the gorge for a further 1km to a second bridge and another path up to Alquézar. The canyon joining the Vero at the Puente de Villacantal is the Barranco de Los Lumos – it is possible to make an exit up this. (Locate a path on the left opposite a tributary canyon. This leads up to the A2205 road midway between Colungo and Lecina.)

2. Barranco de Basender ** 3

Rock	limestone
Length	600m
Descent	110m
Gear	30m rope
Season	all year
Time	approach 40min, descent 1h30, return 30min
Maps	Editorial Alpina: Sierra de Guara II, 1:40,000 Alquézar 30–11, 1:50,000

This dry canyon, a tributary of the Vero, gives an interesting trip through eroded limestone scenery.

Approach

As for the Rio Vero, from the Adahuescar area drive east along the Adahuesca–Arcusa road (A2205) past the Camping Rio Vero and through the village of Colungo. A parking area is reached about 1km before a road junction

Access point:
as for Route 1

Should be dry, may be wet – check the feeder stream before committing to the first long abseil (Route 3)

(left to Lecina left, right to Arcusa). From here, descend to the Rio Vero, cross the bridge, and take a path up the opposite side of the gorge. The path heads south, then south-west, before leading to the gorge entrance after about 1.5km.

Descent

A series of five to seven abseils (one or two short ones are optional) leads to the Rio Vero. At the Vero, go upstream for 0.5km to regain the path and the parking place.

3. Barranco de la Portaicha ** 4-

Rock	limestone
Length	250m
Descent	125m
Gear	2 x 45m rope
Season	all year
Time	approach 30min, descent 1h, return 30min
Maps	Editorial Alpina: Sierra de Guara II, 1:40,000
	Centro Geográfico del Ejército (CGDE): 249 Alquézar 30–11, 1:50,000

This short-but-steep tributary of the Vero lies opposite the Barranco de Basender. Normally dry, it features long, free abseils through spectacular overhanging scenery.

Approach

As for the Rio Vero, drive east along the Adahuesca–Arcusa road (A2205) past the Camping Rio Vero and through the village of Colungo. Follow the road past conglomerate canyons and over the plateau. Park as for Route 1. Walk along the left rim of the Vero gorge, passing a minor tributary canyon, to reach a second tributary, the Portaicha, after 1.5km.

Access point:
as for Route 1

Descent

A long abseil (30m) leads to a flat section. Locate a second abseil, then follow another flat section that gives way to a scrambling descent and another long abseil (35m). Follow a ledge on the right to gain the main gorge of the Rio Vero. Head up this (north) for 1km to a bridge, and gain the path up to the parking place.

4. Barranco de Chimiachas *** 4

Rock	limestone
Length	1.5km
Descent	280m
Gear	2 x 50m rope
Season	all year
Time	approach 1h, descent 3–4h, return 1h30
Maps	Editorial Alpina: Sierra de Guara II, 1:40,000
	Centro Geográfico del Ejército (CGDE): 249 Alquézar 30–11, 1:50,000

This tributary of the Vero gives an excellent and committing descent.

Access point:
about 8km from
Adahuesca

Approach

From Radiquero, a few kilometres west of Alquézar, take a dirt road to San Pelegrín. Pass through the hamlet and go straight ahead to take a right fork (spring here) and find a parking place. Continue on foot, bearing left at path junctions and keeping the summit of Quisals (1130m) on the right. Pass over crags to a ridge, and drop down to gain the head of the canyon.

Descent

A choice of (25–30m) abseil routes in the initial section leads to the canyon floor. Continue past boulders and a series of six shorter abseils to a ledge on the left and another short pitch. Three longer pitches remain before the Rio Vero is reached. Follow the Vero for a few hundred

Arid canyon country
near the Rio Vero

metres, then locate a path that ascends from its right bank, heading roughly west, below south-facing cliffs. After about 1km, a junction with the approach path is reached. Take a left and return to your vehicle. ▶

Variation (Route 4a): continue down the Rio Vero as for Route 1.

5. Barranco de Fornocal *** 3 ≈

Rock	limestone, conglomerate
Length	3km
Descent	150m
Gear	full wetsuit, 25m rope, 2 cars useful
Season	March to October
Time	approach 40min, descent 4h, return 1h
Maps	Editorial Alpina: Sierra de Guara II, 1:40,000
	Centro Geográfico del Ejército (CGDE): 249 Alquézar 30–11,1:50,000

A classic descent with many short abseils and a proliferation of waterfalls and *marmites*. Care is needed when abseiling down waterfalls into pools, especially as this canyon is prone to rapid water build-up after rain.

Access point:
about 17km from
Adahuesca

Approach

As for the Rio Vero, drive east along the Adahuesca–Arcusa road (A2205) past the Camping Rio Vero and through the village of Colungo. The road crosses the Barranco de Fornocal after a few kilometres. Keep driving for a further 4–5km, past the turn-off for the caves at La Mallata, to a dirt road on the right (usually blocked by a barrier). Walk down the road for about 1.5km to where the path divides. Take the right fork which leads to the head of the canyon after a further 1.5km.

Descent

Boulders mark the canyon entrance, which is negotiated by a 12m abseil. Walk down the canyon, passing three short pitches followed by two pitches lying very close together. More waterfall pitches (max 12m) follow, interspersed with ledges and slides. Easy-angled final abseils lead to a pleasant walking section to the Puente La Garganta. Go under the bridge, and scramble up the right bank to the road. Unless you have left a car or are lucky with a lift, an 8km walk awaits.

6. Barranco de las Palomeras ** 3 ≈

Rock	conglomerate
Length	0.35km
Descent	70m
Gear	rope (1 x 25m), wetsuit
Season	January to December
Time	approach 10min, descent 1h30, return 1h
Maps	Editorial Alpina: Sierra de Guara II, 1:40,000
	Centro Geográfico del Ejército (CGDE): 249 Alquézar 30–11, 1:50,000

A short but unique trip through a very narrow cleft into the bowels of the Earth. The stream is sometimes dry, but there are always chest-deep pools in the canyon itself. Recommended for a short, memorable excursion.

Into the gloomy confines of the Barranco de las Palomeras

Access

As for the Rio Vero, drive east along the Adahuesca–Arcusa road (A2205), passing through the village of Colungo. After a few kilometres, the road crosses the

Access point: about 10km from Adahuesca

side-canyon of the Barranco de las Palomeras (sign-posted – if you reach the bridge over the main canyon – the Fornocal – you have gone too far). Park by the bridge. The canyon is reached by a short walk upstream and a careful scramble down.

Descent

Follow the streambed back under the road bridge. There are three short abseils and some moderate squeezes. The canyon develops into a very narrow cleft whose smooth, undulating walls rise high above, almost touching. Wading through narrow pools, emerge into the master canyon of the Fornocal. Turn right and walk upstream almost to the road bridge, where a path scrambles up left to join the road. From here, a stroll of a few minutes leads back to the parking place.

Rodellar area

In the Mascún gorge heading for the Barranco de Otín, accessed via the canyon rim on the left (Route 8)

The Rodellar canyons are every bit as classic as those of the Vero, tending to give long, committing aquatic expeditions. Some are suitable for ropeless days (beginners will appreciate Routes 9, 10 and 12; more experienced canyoners will enjoy Routes 13 and 14), while the true classics of the area, including the Mascún, Otín, Negras and Oscuros de Balcés (Routes 7, 8, 11 and 15), rank with the best in Europe and will be on every canyoner's wish list.

Routes 7–12 all start in the village of Rodellar itself (details in Route 7).

7. Barranco de Mascún Superior **** 4+ ≋

Rock	limestone
Length	2.5km
Descent	140m
Gear	full wetsuit, rope (1 x 50m)
Season	May to November
Time	approach 2h30–3h, descent 3–4h, return 2h
Maps	Editorial Alpina: Sierra de Guara II, 1:40,000
	Centro Geográfico del Ejército (CGDE): 249 Alquézar 30–11, 1:50,000

The Mascún Sup has it all: spectacular scenery, long abseils, dramatic narrows and long swimming sections between soaring rock walls. The narrow sections, as well as being difficult in heavy water flow, see little direct sunlight, and have several abseil pitches where it is easy to lose body heat while retrieving and setting up the ropes and so a full wetsuit is advisable. This is well worth the long approach and fully recommended as one of the classics of the area (if not the planet).

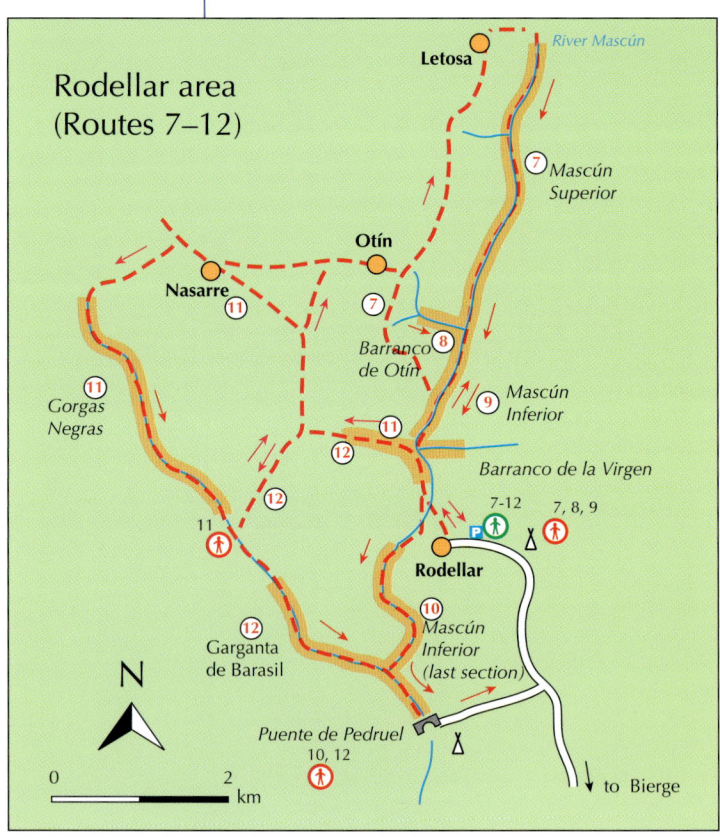

Rodellar area
(Routes 7–12)

River Mascún
Letosa
Mascún Superior ⑦
Otín
Nasarre ⑪
⑦
Barranco de Otín ⑧
⑪ Gorgas Negras
⑪
⑫
Mascún Inferior ⑨
Barranco de la Virgen
7-12 P 7, 8, 9
⑫
11
Rodellar
⑩ Mascún Inferior (last section)
⑫ Garganta de Barasil
N
Puente de Pedruel
10, 12
0   2 km
to Bierge

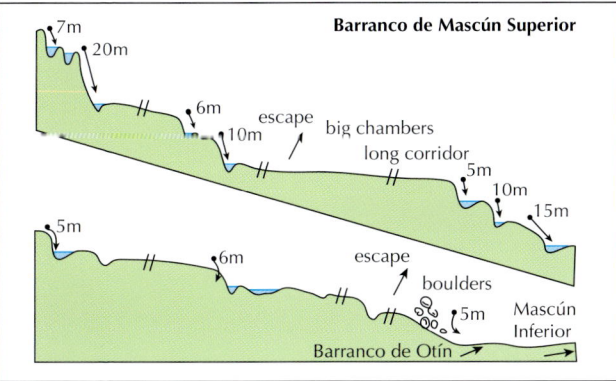

Approach

Park just before Rodellar from where a 5min walk leads to the village church. To the right of the church, a couple of useful signs give details of the local canyons and the path starts here. Descend to the Mascún and walk upstream along the river bed for 1km, to a point where two side-canyons converge on the main gorge. Continue up the main canyon, along the main riverbed, for 1km. Go left before some big limestone spires and head uphill to the plateau and the tiny village of Otín (3km). From here, follow dirt roads north for a further 3km to Letosa, then take the rough road eastwards from here to where it adjoins an insignificant-seeming stream. Follow this down to the head of the gorge, which cuts abruptly into the flat plateau.

Access point:
Rodellar

Descent

Technicalities begin immediately with two abseils (which can be done in one with 2 x 35m ropes) from obvious bolt anchors into waist-high pools. Follow the superb gorge through pools and several narrow water passages, negotiating about ten abseil pitches to join the Mascún Inferior. ▶ The easy subsequent section returns you to familiar territory, the path back up to Rodellar and your car or the campsite.

Don't miss the huge rock spires here – look behind you!

Bang into a deep pool, Mascún Superior

In the narrows of the Barranco de Mascún Superior

8. Barranco de Otín *** 4+

Rock	limestone
Length	500m
Descent	240m
Gear	ropes (2 x 45m), full wetsuit
Season	January to December
Time	approach 2h30, descent 2h30, return 1h30
Maps	Editorial Alpina: Sierra de Guara II, 1:40,000
	Centro Geográfico del Ejército (CGDE): 249 Alquézar 30–11, 1:50,000

An area classic, involving several long free abseils amid impressive rock scenery. Usually dry later in the season. To get a feel for it, visit the 'Explorations' section of the Petzl Sport website (http://en.petzl.com/petzl/SportAccueil) and choose Canyoning/Barranco de Otín.

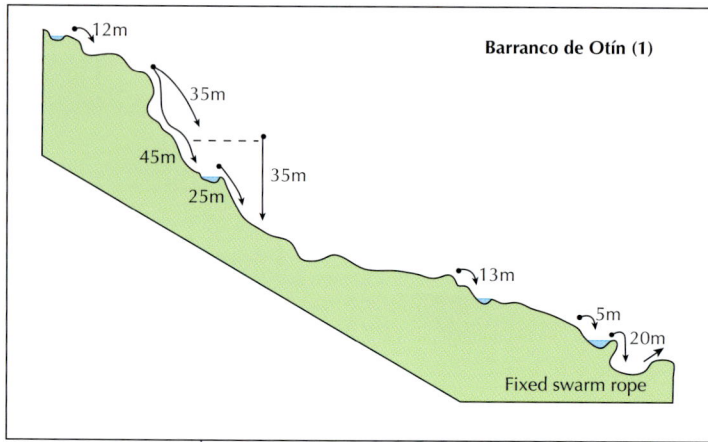

Barranco de Otín (1)

12m

35m

45m

35m

25m

13m

5m

20m

Fixed swarm rope

Access point:
Rodellar

Approach

From Rodellar, take the path by the church that heads down into the Mascún gorge and head upstream past a three-way canyon junction to gain a path on the left (true right bank) that makes a zigzag ascent to the plateau. Locate the head of the canyon on the right, about 1km before the village of Otín.

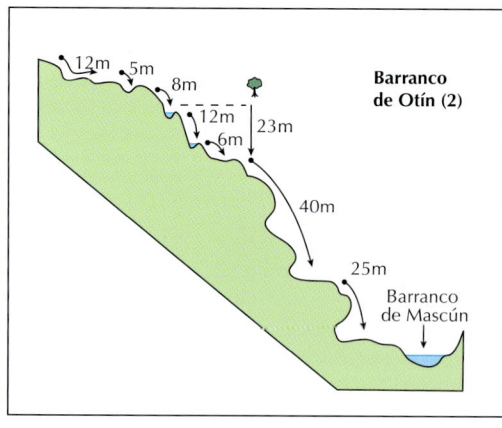

Barranco de Otín (2)

12m   5m

8m

12m

6m   23m

40m

25m

Barranco de Mascún

Guara canyoning at its best – near the junction of the Mascún and the Barranco de Otín

Descent
A short abseil (12m), made from an anchor on the right, precedes a second long, free pitch and a third shorter pitch. Stow the ropes for a boulder-hopping section prior to a couple of shorter pitches. A descent is made into a dry pothole, from which an escape is made using a fixed rope. A few more pitches precede the final overhanging abseils. Clamber past boulders to the master gorge of the Mascún. The easy subsequent section returns you to familiar territory, the path back up to Rodellar and your car or the campsite.

9. Barranco de Mascún Inferior ** 1

Rock	limestone
Length	3.5km
Ascent/descent	50m
Gear	short wetsuit, or shorts and T-shirt on a hot day
Season	March to October
Time	approach 2h30, descent 2h30, return 15min
Maps	Editorial Alpina: Sierra de Guara II, 1:40,000
	Centro Geográfico del Ejército (CGDE): 249 Alquézar 30–11, 1:50,000

This relaxed, easy canyon has great views of the Mascún limestone cliffs and spires, and consists of hiking and wading, with pools, boulders and pot-holes adding spice. A wetsuit will add to the fun, but you can easily avoid a soaking.

Access and descent
Access point:
Rodellar

From Rodellar take the path by the church that heads down into the Mascún gorge. Follow the gorge upstream as far as your inclination allows. The way is blocked when the Mascún Superior is reached, first by a boulder choke and then by a short pitch. Return the same way.

The crags of the Mascún Inferior are well known for tufa formations and steep climbing (credit: Guy Maddox)

The descent into the Mascún from the village of Rodellar (Routes 7–12)

10. Barranco de Mascún Inferior – last section * 2 ∿

Rock	limestone
Length	1.7km
Descent	30m
Gear	short wetsuit
Season	March to October
Time	approach 15min, descent 2h, return 1h
Maps	Editorial Alpina: Sierra de Guara II, 1:40,000
	Centro Geográfico del Ejército (CGDE): 249 Alquézar 30–11, 1:50,000

This is the section of the Mascún that leads downstream from Rodellar to join the Barrasil at a long, unavoidable pool. A very pleasant outing.

Access
From Rodellar take the path by the church that heads down into the Mascún gorge. Turn left to follow the stream down the bed of the gorge.

Access point:
Rodellar

Descent
Hike and wade down the canyon for about 1.5km. An unavoidable pool gives a long, atmospheric swimming section that junctions with the lower section of the Barrasil. Turn left and, eventually, emerge from the pool. A short hike leads to the elegant arched bridge of Puente de Pedruel, and perhaps some refreshment if the neighbouring campsite bar is open. Should more action be required, there is a short-but-fun *via ferrata* up on the left. Otherwise, a steep walk up the road leads back to Rodellar (2km).

Walking the initial approach section to the Gorgas Negras, up the Mascún Inferior

11. Gorgas Negras *** 4 ≋

Rock	limestone
Length	4.5km
Descent	150m
Gear	rope (1 x 30m), wetsuit
Season	June to October
Time	approach 2h30, descent 4h30 (+ Barrasil (2h)), return 1h
Maps	Editorial Alpina: Sierra de Guara II, 1:40,000
	Centro Geográfico del Ejército (CGDE): 249 Alquézar 30–11, 1:50,000

Another Guara classic, this gives a long and committing expedition best combined with the Garganta de Barrasil which lies downstream. There are no torrents and you should be able to keep your walking clothes (T-shirt, shorts and so on) dry in plastic bags in a small rucksack during the canyon descent.

Access

Access point:
Rodellar

Take the path descending into the Mascún gorge (see Route 7) and head upstream along the meandering riverbed for 1km, to a point where two side-canyons converge on the main gorge. Take the left-hand canyon, following an enchanting dry streambed that weaves its way through dense thickets of trees and bushes to emerge onto a ridge (1h). Take the right fork of the path that leads up to the plateau and the village of Otín, but leave the path at the Dolmen Losa Mora and follow another path in a north-westerly direction to the village of Nasarre (1191m). The peak of Lupera (1467 m) is on your left. Go past the village, then take a left fork and descend to the river and the head of the canyon.

Descent

The first section includes short abseils and boulder sections that give way to steeper fare and bigger pools. A long chaotic waterway follows for about 1.5km, prior to further abseils amid chaotic boulder chokes. Follow the streambed to where the valley opens out. At this point it is possible to walk over to the Mascún and Rodellar, although it's more satisying to continue down the Barrasil (Route 12) for the full experience and a grand day out.

12. Garganta de Barrasil ** 2+ ≋

Rock	limestone
Length	2.5km
Descent	60m
Gear	wetsuit
Season	May to November
Time	approach 1h30, descent 2–3h, return 1h
Maps	Editorial Alpina: Sierra de Guara II, 1:40,000
	Centro Geográfico del Ejército (CGDE): 249 Alquézar 30–11, 1:50,000

This easy but dramatic canyon is a lot of fun. It culminates in a long, unavoidable swim through a deep pool, possible without a wetsuit for hardy commando types. There are no torrents and you should be able to keep your walking clothes (T-shirt, shorts and so on) dry in a small rucksack during the canyon descent.

Access point:
Rodellar

Approach
Begin with a beautiful walk starting near the church in Rodellar (see Route 7). Take the path descending into the Mascún gorge, and head upstream along the meandering riverbed for 1km, to a point where two side-canyons converge on the main gorge. Take the left-hand canyon, following the dry streambed that weaves its way through dense thickets of trees and bushes to emerge onto a ridge (1h). Here, do not take the right fork of the path that leads up to the village of Otín; instead, go over the ridge following the path that descends to join the river

Alcanadre at an easy, wide section, below a dramatic and more difficult section upstream (Gorgas Negras).

Deep in one of the Barrasil's narrow sections

Descent
The first part of the descent is an easy walk, and you can change into your wetsuit as and when you please. Wading, hiking and scrambling, with the odd slide to tempt you in the main streambed, lead downstream to the first of a series of large pools. Swim across the first one and progress on foot amid increasingly interesting canyon scenery with great chaotic cliffs on the left bank. A long, unavoidable swimming channel is soon reached, where the dark water flows gently and quietly between limestone walls that become increasingly enclosed. This final, long swimming section has a superbly serene feel, and a detour into the lower section of the Mascún Inferior (junction on the left) is possible. Emerging from the pool, more wading and hiking lead to the bridge of Puente de Pedruel which marks the end of the gorge. Walk up the road past a campsite to regain the main road and Rodellar (2km), or for added interest, try the minuscule *via ferrata* on the left bank above the bridge.

81

13. Garganta de la Peonara Superior *** 2+

Rock	limestone
Length	4.5km
Descent	100m
Gear	wetsuit
Season	May to October
Time	approach 30min, descent 3–4h, return 1h
Maps	Editorial Alpina: Sierra de Guara II, 1:40,000
	Centro Geográfico del Ejército (CGDE): 249 Alquézar 30–11, 1:50,000

Fine walking, wading and swimming through some dramatic scenery. The gorge weaves its mysterious way between cliffs of ever-increasing magnitude, while the swimming sections range from serene and relaxing to narrow and exciting. A long and fairly strenuous outing that feels quite remote, and gives a great day out.

Access point: about 9km from Rodellar

Access

From Rodellar, drive about 8km south (A1227) and turn right to San Saturnino (signposted). Park before the farm buildings and walk down the dirt track to the river.

Descent

Head downstream – easy walking at first, reminiscent of Chee Dale in the Peak District. The gorge meanders pleasantly towards deep and narrow sections, where the descent becomes very aquatic with long swimming sections. Keep hiking, swimming and hiking for about 4.5km, the last section becoming quite tiring as you wade the riverbed. The escape path weaves up slopes on the left, opposite a huge orange cliff, and is marked by a small cairn with red paint on the left bank. Just before it is a stone wall that is easy to spot on the right bank (about 4h to here). The energetic may wish to continue

Afloat in the Peonara Sup

Once more into the pool, Peonara Sup

the descent to the Peonara Inferior (Route 14); others must face the steep hike to the east rim of the gorge. On the opposite (west) side is a hermitage nestling beneath the cliff – the Pared de San Martin – which comes into view as you gain altitude. Follow the path and reach the road about an hour from the gorge bed. It's 3–4km back to your car but you might get a lift at the main road if you're lucky.

14. Garganta de la Peonara Inferior *** 3 ≈

Rock	limestone
Length	2.5km
Descent	60m
Gear	wetsuit
Season	May to November
Time	approach 40min, descent 3h30, return 1h
Maps	Editorial Alpina: Sierra de Guara II, 1:40,000
	Centro Geográfico del Ejército (CGDE): 249 Alquézar 30–11, 1:50,000

A great canyon, featuring lots of water passages, boulder sections, slides and jumps. Both the walk-in and walk-out are also very pleasant. Could be appended to the Peonara Superior depending on transport and an inclination for a very long day.

Easy walking in the Peonara

Access point:
about 20km from
Rodellar

Access

Start and finish near the ghost-like village of Morrano, which is on the west side of the Peonara, about 6km from Bierge. Park in a well-marked area by a bend in the road to the north of the village. A good dirt road leads through woodland to the gorge, which is fairly open here, beneath larger enclosing crags further upstream. Decent paths lead down the streambed and give the option of missing out the first meander, which loops around clockwise.

Descent

Follow the watercourse through a steep-sided defile, with plenty of swimming and increasing interest. At the end of the canyon, which is over all too soon, a path leads up to the right. Follow this up to Morrano, passing an impressive conglomerate cliff with a huge tower, making a right when you hit the road to take you back to your car. Alternatively, continue downstream to the long water passage of the Gorges de Puntillo (** 3 〰), which emerges on the Bierge–Morrano road (for this, two cars would be preferable).

15. Oscuros de Balcés **** 4 〰

Rock	limestone
Length	1.5km
Descent	50m
Gear	full wetsuit, rope (1 x 20m)
Season	May to November
Time	approach 1h, descent 2h30, return 1h
Maps	Editorial Alpina: Sierra de Guara II, 1:40,000
	Centro Geográfico del Ejército (CGDE): 249 Alquézar 30–11, 1:50,000

An excellent, committing expedition with labyrinthine sections of huge boulders, and a long narrow passage involving swimming and wading between vertical rock walls that are only a few metres apart.

Access

Start at the dirt road that leads along the ridge from the Rodellar road a few kilometres south of Las Almunias. Drive along the dirt road until a barrier bars the way and park here. Walk to the end of the dirt road, then contour right along a rocky path that eventually goes around a ridge high above the gorge. Continue at the same level amid dramatic scenery, until the path drops steeply down to the valley floor (1h).

Access point:
about 10km from Rodellar

Descent

Easy walking and wading leads back south to the jaws of the canyon. Soon, aquatic sections among huge boulders pose an interesting route-finding challenge (first abseil points hidden up on the left). Care is needed with slippery rock and fast-flowing water in the maze. Soon the narrows are reached, and the passage becomes incredibly atmospheric and noisy. More inventive route-finding is needed to locate abseil anchors, and a second short abseil follows into a very narrow section. ▸

NB: The water here can be very powerful.

Swim to the next short abseil, which may be hazardous if in spate (short rope recommended). Try to use the anchors out on the right wall to stay out of the waterfall, and, once floating, pay out rope to escape the deluge. Easy pools and slides lead to a point where the gorge opens out and changes character, with red conglomerate cliffs coming in from the right. Here, an exit path winds up through the woodland on the right. Follow this back up to your car. Alternatively, if energy and time allow, take the continuation canyon of the Estrechos de Balcés (Route 16) deep into conglomerate country.

16. Estrechos de Balcés * 2

Rock	conglomerate
Length	6.5km

Descent	100m
Gear	wetsuit
Season	May to November
Time	approach 40min, descent 4–5h, return 15km by road
Maps	Editorial Alpina: Sierra de Guara II, 1:40,000
	Centro Geográfico del Ejército (CGDE): 249 Alquézar 30–11, 1:50,000

This gorge, contiguous with the Oscuros doe Balcés (Route 15), comprises a long walk and wade in interesting conglomerate country. Many worthwhile side-canyons form short but committing excursions hereabouts, and this canyon forms their easy escape route.

Access point:
about 10km from
Rodellar

Approach

If you have two cars, leave one at the village of Albuerela de la Liena; if not hitching is a possibility. Either way, start at the dirt road that leads along the ridge from the Rodellar road a few kilometres south of Las Almunias, as for Route 15. Head along the dirt road until a barrier bars the way and park here, where a path on the right drops down to the valley floor, joining the watercourse just downstream of the Oscuros de Balcés (Route 15).

Descent

Follow the gorge, passing some impressive limestone arch features on the left, on foot or afloat as conditions dictate. At some length, during which at least 12 well-documented side-canyons join the master gorge, the canyon relents near the village of Albuerela de la Liena. Here gain the road, and, unless you have left a support vehicle, hitch to Bierge and then back up towards Rodellar and your car.

Conglomerate towers, home to dozens of Lammergeier, near the Barranco de Yara

17. Rio Formiga – Barranco de Yara ** 3 ≋

Rock	conglomerate
Length	1.5km
Descent	60m
Gear	wetsuit, rope (1 x 25m)
Season	May to November. Best early in the season when there is more water.
Time	approach 1h, descent 2h, return 15min
Maps	Editorial Alpina: Sierra de Guara II, 1:40,000
	Centro Geográfico del Ejército (CGDE): 249 Alquézar 30–11, 1:50,000

On the margins of the Rodellar region, this canyon lies in stupendous conglomerate country that becomes even more extensive further west. A narrow channel that is best in above-average conditions of water flow.

Access point:
about 25km from
Rodellar

Access
By road (A1227) from Bierge, pass through the villages of Morrano, Yaso and Bastaras. A few kilometres past Bastaras, park in a large layby at a loop in the road by a bridge. There is a useful sign showing canyon details at the car park. A hike through pleasant forest leads to the gorge, where a path up the northern side of the valley gradually gains an exposed ledge system on an imposing cliff-side, amid interesting geology. Carefully traverse the ledges until an abseil station is reached slightly down to the left. Three short abseils and some scrambling allow access to the streambed.

Descent
Follow the confines of the canyon with interest, passing boulders, pools and a few short abseils. At the end of the difficulties, the gorge eases back into walking territory. Follow the approach path back to the car park.

COSTA BLANCA

The Costa Blanca lies on Spain's eastern, Mediterranean coast, roughly between Valencia in the north and Alicante in the south. The area hosts several fine canyons of which the Barranco del Infierno is by far the best known, and for good

The Barranc de l'Estret de Penyes – an abrupt exit into cultivated terraces (Route 20)

Costa Blanca
Routes 18–23

reason. This canyon has an otherworldly, almost claustrophobic atmosphere, characterised by large round swirl-pots, or *marmites*, of bright white limestone. These form a series of obstacles that may contain various amounts of water, or none at all, in which case each pot will be seen to contain a bed of meticulously stone-washed pebbles that might have been imported from a beach. The Infierno is great fun, requires no specialist equipment and should not be missed if conditions allow, which is most of the time.

On the whole the other canyons in the area are relatively short and sweet, taking a few hours at most. Although they are not up to the standard of the Barranco del Infierno, some are rather fine with narrow channels, good clear water, and interesting features. They are definitely worth a detour if you are in the area and need a break from your climbing, walking or sunbathing schedule, and are at their best in the spring months. A car is pretty much essential for getting to any of the canyons in the area.

Practicalities
Getting there
Alicante is the gateway to the Costa Blanca and the package holiday paradise of Benidorm. Ryanair fly from Liverpool and London (daily), Dublin (five times a week), East Midlands (four times a week), and Bournemouth and Doncaster (three times a week); EasyJet fly from Bristol, Belfast, Liverpool, Newcastle, Luton, Stansted, Nottingham and Gatwick; British Midland fly from Birmingham, Cardiff,

Calpe's unique rock peninsula – the Peñón d'Ifach, Costa Blanca

It's cheap, it's clean, it's handy, it's grotesque...it's Benidorm

Durham, Heathrow, Manchester and Nottingham; Flybe fly from Birmingham, Exeter, Norwich and Southampton; and British Airways also offers regular flights from London Gatwick. Over the peak summer season, charter airlines often offer the cheapest flights: Monarch go from Birmingham, Luton, Manchester and Gatwick, and Thomsonfly from Bournemouth, Birmingham, Cardiff, Coventry, Glasgow, Doncaster, Luton, Gatwick, Manchester, Nottingham and Newcastle. In addition, Air Scotland (www.air-scotland.com) has a few flights to Alicante from Edinburgh and Glasgow, and Aer Lingus (www.aerlingus.com) has flights from Dublin and Cork.

Alicante airport (tel: (+34) 966 919 000 or 100) is located seven miles (11km) south of Alicante. For transfer to the city, regular buses leave every 30 minutes for the main bus station in Alicante. Rail travel along the coastal belt or from Madrid is also a feasible way to get to the region (details at the RENFE timetable website: www.renfe.es)

Getting around
A car is almost essential for getting to the Costa Blanca canyons. Try searching on the internet for Jet Car, Holiday Autos or Sun Cars, or try: www.rent.it or www.holidayautos.co.uk.

When to go

Descent of all the canyons, including the Barranco del Infierno, is possible all year. Most are essentially dry all year round and are normally descended when no water is flowing – therefore, be very wary of any water flow in these 'dry' canyons. The exceptions are the Barranco de Melo and the Barranc de L'Estret de Penyes, where clear flowing water – and so more challenge – should be found in the spring than later in the season.

Where to stay

Self-catering accommodation can be booked easily and cheaply before leaving home. A useful site for apartments, right up to last-minute booking, is www.hotelsabroad.co.uk. The magazine *Private Villas* lists properties with UK owners and their contact numbers. For information on all sorts of accommodation options try www.costablanca.org.

A high-rise in Benidorm is often the easiest option and can be incredibly cheap, especially if you're splitting the cost of an apartment between several people. However, parking can be a problem so make sure that it is covered in the cost. Benidorm is clean and surprisingly pleasant, at least in the off-season, and is chock-full of cheap food and drink. However, it's almost been annexed by the British retirement contingent, and it can be difficult to find a Spanish bar simply to drink a coffee in. Also, Benidorm can be a hassle in the rush hour. If your instincts

A typical Costa Blanca mountain path
(Route 18) (credit: The Orange House)

COSTA BLANCA ROUTES	Grade	Quality	Rock	Length (km)	De
18. Barranco del Infierno	3 〰	***	L	1.0	
19. Barranc del Sant/Barranco de Melo	1/3	– / *	L	0.3/0.8	40/1
20. Barranc de l'Estret de Penyes	2+	**	L	0.3	
21. Barranco de Soler	3	*	L	800.0	3
22. Barranco de les Raboses	1+	*	L	0.3	
23. Barranco de Relleu	2+	**	L	0.8	1
L – limestone					

are more for rural solitude then you'll be better off elsewhere. Alternatives in the form of apartments or villas from Alicante right up to Gandia are fairly easy to organise.

The Sella-Finestrat area is convenient for most of the canyons and there is a friendly, basic mountain refuge near the crags at Sella itself (Casa Refugio, Font de l'Arc, 03579 Sella, Alicante, Spain, tel: (+34) 965 941 019), although camping is no longer an option here. The Orange House in Finestrat is a handy place to stay and extremely pleasant especially if you're looking for climbing company or you want to hire a guide for canyoning or climbing (www.theorangehouse.net).

There are numerous campsites to be found in behind the coastal strip, although many are generally geared to the beach holiday crowd and are often expensive. They are usually closed in the winter and crowded in summer. Reputedly, there is a good, affordable campsite at Olta (just above Calpe, go past the railway station and follow the signs), with good facilities and a superb position. There are several youth hostels up and down the coast and in the towns further inland.

Maps and guides

The Michelin map Costa Blanca, (123 Zoom; 1:130,000) is a good road map that should enable you to locate the canyons described. (The one you want has a green cover – make sure you get this one and not the red 1:300,000 one. It is available at the huge Carrefour supermarket between Finestrat and Benidorm and at newsagents). The official maps (CGDE 821 Alcoy 29–32, 822 Benisa 30–32, 846 Ibi 28–33 and 847 Villajoyosa 29–33) cover the canyon areas but are less easy to get hold of and of limited use as paths are generally not marked. For specific canyons there are some details available on the web, but they tend to be incomplete. Useful sites include: www.barranquismo.net/buscador/espana and the increasingly comprehensive www.descente-canyon.com.

ason	Time	Gear (optional/seasonal)		Access
year	4hr45–5hr45	rope (wetsuit)		car
year	1hr30/2hr30–3hr30	rope/rope, wetsuit		car
year	2hr30	rope, wetsuit		car
year	3hr–3hr30	rope		1–2 cars
year	1hr	rope		car
year	3hr45	rope, wetsuit		2 cars

Other activities

From September to May the Costa Blanca offers some of the best winter walking in Europe. The area has spectacular trails – a combination of mountain tracks, farm lanes and old Mozarabic paths which link the small villages of the interior. There are several guides in print (including Bob Stanfield's very good *Costa Blanca Mountain Walks* (in two volumes), Cicerone Press). There is good walking and ridge scrambling on the Bernia ridge directly west of Calpe and accessed via Pinos from Benissa. The Costa Blanca is an established rock climbing destination and the quality of the routes and variety of crags that are peppered all over the area is superb. The best guide to these is published by Rockfax.

THE ROUTES

The Costa Blanca canyons, dotted about the region and isolated from each other, differ widely in character but are nevertheless all at the small end of the spectrum. None of them have the grandeur of the Guara or Verdon canyons, but you will certainly get away from it all in the amazing Infierno (Route 18) and the Relleu (Route 23). The semi-urban Estret de Penyes and Soller (Routes 19 and 21) may not be to everyone's taste, at least until you are deep within them and so oblivious to their surroundings. Of the technical canyons, some are very easy and short, making them especially suitable for beginners, for example the Sant and the Raboses (Routes 19 and 22). All the canyons are cut into a bedrock of excellent, fine-grained limestone and have interesting rock formations.

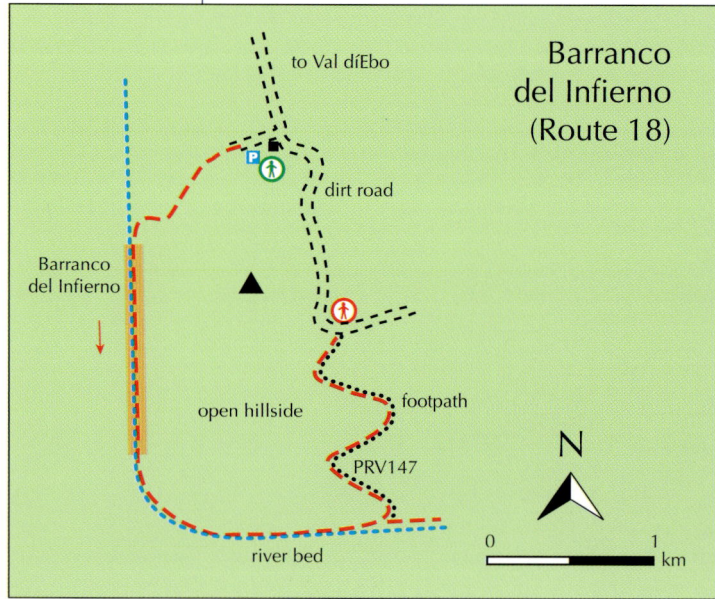

18. Barranco del Infierno *** 3 〰

Length	1km
Descent	80m
Gear	30m rope, a few extra krabs and slings, wetsuit not usually needed
Season	January to December
Time	approach 45min, descent 2–3h, return 2h
Maps	Michelin Costa Blanca road map (123 Zoom; 1:130,000)
	CGDE: 821 Alcoy 29-32; 822 Benisa 30-32; 846 Ibi 28-33; 847 Villajoyosa 29-33 (all 1:50,000)

A superb, exciting outing through a series of unique rounded *marmites*, formed in wonderfully sculpted white limestone. The gorge is fully equipped with abseil anchors, and several fixed swarm ropes and traverse cables are in place. There are about ten abseil pitches, plus perhaps one or two very short ones if ropes are not

Traversing fixed cables in the Barranco del Infierno (credit: The Orange House)

If the river is flowing, which is rare, the seriousness of the outing becomes substantially higher, and you will definitely need a wetsuit.

in place. Descent is straightforward if the canyon is dry, but the serial *marmite* formations can fill with water. **Be prepared for some technical ropework on fixed cables if this is the case.** Some pools fill to a depth of a few feet, deeper after prolonged periods of rain, when being in the depths of the gorge can be cold experience without a wetsuit. ◀ Indeed, in these conditions, you may run out of daylight and there have been fatalities (including drownings).

Access

Access point: about 1hr drive from Calpe

From the Calpe area, follow the A7 motorway towards Valencia and turn off at Denia (Junction 62). Go north on the N332, through Ondara, for 5km, then turn left for Pego (CV700) which is reached after a further 11.5km. From Pego take the CV715 towards Sagra and Orba, but just outside Pego turn right and follow signs to la Val d'Ebo, reached by a long, winding mountain road (CV712). At the top (Passo de Manzanera) near a windmill-like structure, well before you get to the main village, turn left down a tarmac and dirt track. After 4km turn right (signposted Les Juvées Denmig) and park by some ruined buildings 100m down on the left. From here, a path leads to the north side of the gorge.

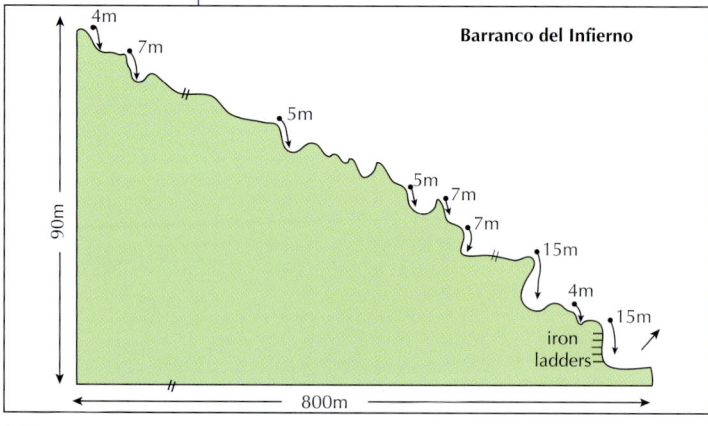

One of the many marmites deep in the Barranco del Infierno (credit: The Orange House)

Descent

A steep path finds its way down a craggy side-canyon, before opening out to a slope, and onto the bed of the gorge proper. Follow the riverbed into a rocky downstream section, where the first of many gravel-bedded *marmites* will appear. Hereabouts, fixed ropes are often *in situ*, allowing descent on one side and ascent on the other. As the route continues, the *marmites* tend to become wider, deeper, and more impressive and a few short abseils will become necessary. The first of these is into a big *marmite* that seems a formidable obstacle but is actually quite easy when dry. If a traverse is made along the fixed cables on the right wall to avoid deep water, krabs, slings and perhaps belaying skills will be needed. A slabby face forms the exit and some scrambling or climbing efforts may be needed if no fixed rope is in place. Continue in the same vein to a large cave with some ladders fixed from below, after which the narrows of the gorge are passed and it suddenly opens out into walking territory.

Continue down the rocky streambed, which veers to the left for about 20 minutes until you hit a track crossing the valley (the PRV147). Head up left, where zigzags lead past a well to a dirt road and the terrain levels off. Continue up the road and take a left turn to the parking space to return to your car.

*19. Barranc del Sant/Barranco de Melo * 1/3*

Length	300m/800m
Descent	40m/140m
Gear	rope (1 x 20m)/rope (1 x 50m) plus wetsuit
Season	January to December
Time	1h30 return, Sant only; 3–4h for both canyons
Maps	Michelin Costa Blanca road map (123 Zoom; 1:130,000)
	CGDE: 821 Alcoy 29-32; 822 Benisa 30-32; 846 Ibi 28-33; 847 Villajoyosa 29-33 (all 1:50,000)

These routes are, in reality, two sections of the same canyon that have traditionally been divided due to their differences in character. Both can be done at any time of year, and are essentially dry in conditions of drought, but the Melo is at its best outside these times when the water will be clear and clean (and cold – wetsuit advised). The first section (the Sant) is open, ill-defined and escapable: all the difficulties including pools and abseil pitches can be bypassed, and you can wade or make short abseils into pools (if present) as desired, making it an easy proposition suitable for children or beginners. The second section (the Melo), enclosed and much superior, is more aquatic, especially if in spate.

Access

From the hilltop castle of Guadalest (CV70 from Benidorm or CV755 from Altea/Calpe) head towards Alcoy for about 7km and, before arriving at Confrides, take a right turn towards Abdet and park in the main car park past the village. At the top of the car park is a small road that continues out of town heading north. Follow

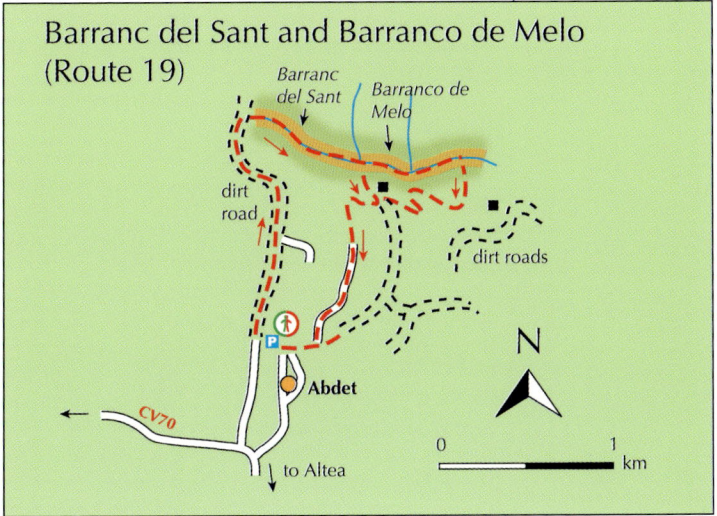

Barranc del Sant and Barranco de Melo
(Route 19)

Barranc del Sant

Barranco de Melo

dirt road

dirt roads

N

Abdet

← CV70

to Altea

0   1
          km

The Barranc del Sant in semi-dry conditions

this over a ridge, passing olive terraces until the road crosses an unimpressive watercourse – the top of the gorge (10min).

Descent

Work down the gorge for about 300m passing small obstacles and vegetated sections with a few short abseils. Where the gorge begins to show some interesting bedrock features, a prominent roofed barn becomes easily visible on the rim on the right. An escape can be made up slopes to the barn. From here, work along the terraces to find tracks taking you back to the village and its car park (1–2h round trip).

Alternatively, to continue from the foot of this escape route, down the Barranco de Melo, continue past the first of a series of pools into the gorge proper, which narrows to form a series of atmospheric pools. There are several short pitches, some of which can be jumped (be careful to send someone down first to check the water depth!). Where the gorge opens out, escape up the steep, wooded slope to the right to locate another house (invisible from below) and walk uphill past terraces back to the village. In total, this stage comprises eight or nine easy abseils (mostly 8–12m, maximum 27m if some are linked). ▶

The adventurous may wish to continue down the gorge's lower reaches, into the relatively unknown.

20. Barranc de l'Estret de Penyes ** 2+

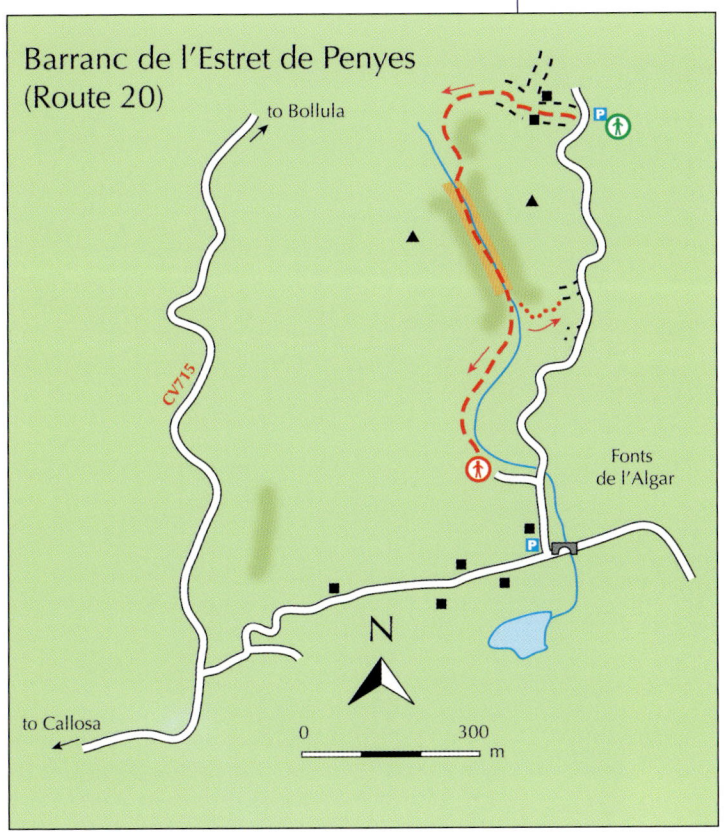

Barranc de l'Estret de Penyes
(Route 20)

to Bollula

CV715

Fonts
de l'Algar

to Callosa

N

0   300
        m

Length	300m
Descent	40m
Gear	rope (1 x 50m), wetsuit needed most of the year
Season	January to December
Time	2–2h15 (access 35min; descent 1h15; return 30min)
Maps	Michelin Costa Blanca road map (123 Zoom; 1:130,000)
	CGDE: 821 Alcoy 29-32; 822 Benisa 30-32; 846 Ibi 28-33; 847 Villajoyosa 29-33 (all 1:50,000)

A great little canyon with extremely clear water, especially early in the year and after rains. Moderate water flow is likely at most times of year, with pools of up to 2m deep, although the gorge can dry out at times. The gorge itself is wild enough but its environs are heavily cultivated and many tiny roads and tracks can make it hard to find. **Follow the directions carefully.**

Access point:
about 20mins drive
from Calpe

Access

From Altea (CV755) or Benidorm (CV70) head to Callosa. At the central roundabout take the CV715 towards Bollula, picking up signs for the Fonts d'Algar (a popular waterfall area). After about 2km, turn right towards the Fonts d'Algar, passing into a heavily cultivated fruit-growing valley. After 1.1km, just before a little bridge amid several restaurants and parking areas, turn left (if you start to go uphill past the Fonts you have gone too far). Go straight up this narrow road for exactly 1km until you reach the first of several large silver telegraph poles at a road junction. Park here (room for one or two cars only).

Gear up, and walk along the dirt road on the left, soon passing between two sheds. At the first hairpin (about 200m from your car), turn left onto another dirt road leading along a terrace to a lone olive tree at its end. Follow a footpath downhill through disused terraces for another 300m, passing along the bottom of an excellent-looking bolted crag (worth a look for interested climbers – no route details known but recently developed with a wide range of grades). Below the end of the crag, the jaws of the canyon emerge through the trees.

Crystal-clear water in the Barranc de l'Estret de Penyes

Descent

The first abseil (8m) leads to interesting gorge features in the depths of a narrow defile with steep, high walls. Beautifully carved scoops and basins lead with interest down the canyon for about 300m. All too soon the outflow is reached, where the terrain changes dramatically into a cultivated valley in which the hand of man is overwhelmingly evident.

The main 20m abseil is found here. There is **danger in spate** as the line of the abseil is directly in the water flow but there are alternative anchors high on the right that are safer in spate conditions. (It is also possible to escape along the water conduit on the right, where a long diversion through private land leads through interesting orange and lemon groves.) From the basin below, head through bamboo for a few metres and follow the stream or terraced banks. Another alternative exit, avoiding private land, is feasible by heading up through terraces on the hillside on the left. Rejoin the road near the restaurants, and walk back up the road to your car (1.1km).

21. Barranco de Soler * 3

Length	800m
Descent	300m
Gear	rope (1 x 60m or 1 x 50m if careful)
Season	January to December
Time	1h30–2h, return 1h30 unless you have another vehicle
Maps	Michelin Costa Blanca road map (123 Zoom; 1:130,000)
	CGDE: 821 Alcoy 29-32; 822 Benisa 30-32; 846 Ibi 28-33; 847 Villajoyosa 29-33 (all 1:50,000)

This canyon has some long abseils and is rated by some as second best to the Barranco del Infierno as local canyons go. Although it has good water-worn features and is well worthwhile, the Soler lacks the memorable atmosphere of the Infierno and is let down by its proximity to built-up areas and the brevity of its interesting lower section. However, you can drive right to the top, and, after finishing the descent, the walk back uphill is surprisingly pleasant, if a little complicated. Unless you masochistically insist on a directissima descent, mimicking the fall of a drop of water from start to finish, the gorge can usually be done dry except for the pool at the very bottom, which is in any case avoidable. However, it's advisable to take some krabs and slings for traversing in case the potholes are full of water. Climbers may note that this gorge is on the same rocky hillside as the Alcoy crag (see the Rockfax guide to Costa Blanca).

Access

From the Benidorm area, access to the town of Alcoy is probably easiest via Alicante and the N340, rather than the winding mountain road past Guadalest that looks more direct on the map. From Alcoy, take the road to Banyeres (CV795: just as you leave Alcoy, on the right, is a road (Carrer del Mestre Ribera Motes) that leads to a bridge. This marks the end of the gorge. If you have a spare vehicle, leave it here). A few kilometres up the Banyeres road you pass through a tunnel. Take the second right after the tunnel, signposted Preventori, and follow this road for 2.8km until you reach a bar, some public toilets, an electricity substation and a parking area. There are great views over Alcoy, if urban sprawl is your thing.

Access point:
about 1hr 30mins drive from Calpe

Descent

Descend the steps and follow the right bank of the watercourse, which looks distinctly unappealing. The first abseil passes rather pointlessly over brambles into a deep pond but may appeal to urban guerrillas and commando types. Level-headed individuals will avoid this on the right, pondering the absence of recognisably canyonesque features. Do not despair – things will soon improve!

Head down through trees to an open cliff, which is abseiled direct (although, again, it can easily be avoided

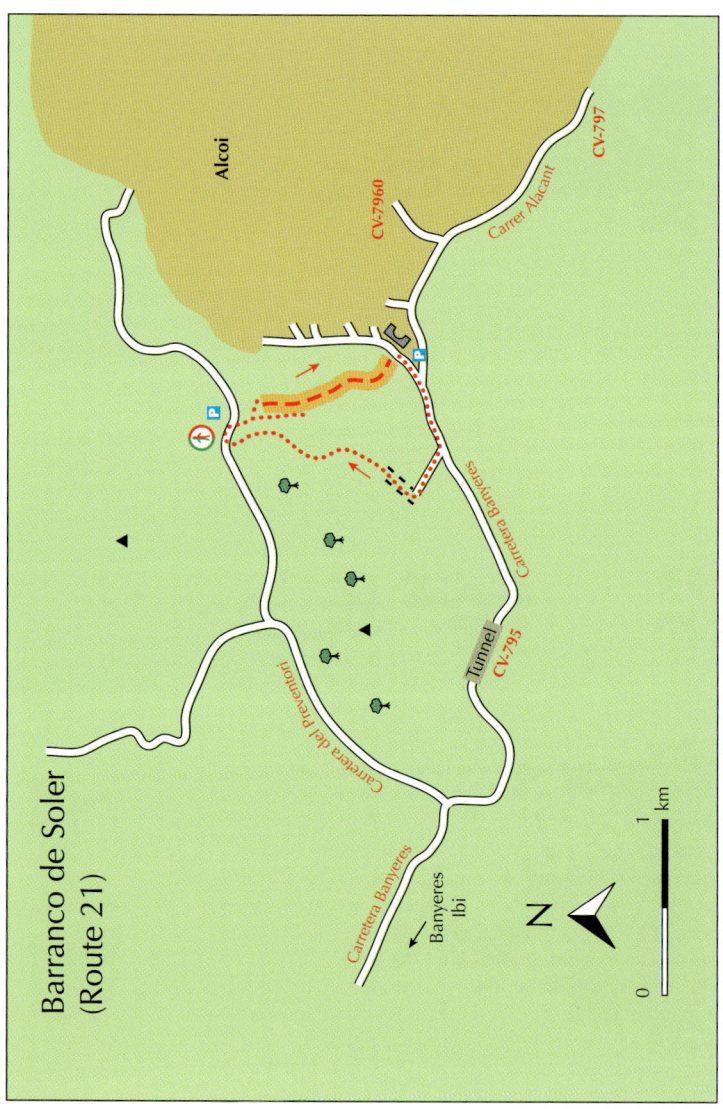

Barranco de Soler
(Route 21)

on the right). There are several anchors, the higher ones requiring at least a 60m rope (if you only have a 50m rope, look out for the halfway anchor; or it is *just* possible to get to the highest part of the ledge below). Wander down through vegetation until, with some relief, you enter the canyon proper. Descend this with several raps past interesting *marmites*, many of which seem to contain odd shoes.

To avoid abseiling into the last pool, you can cross the void on a taut fixed cable. This provides a thrilling zip-wire Tyrolian traverse, so long as you don't mind smacking into a huge tree at high speed and going to hospital. Better to abseil into the pool. A scramble off to the left is also possible but quite tricky, especially if you are under six foot tall. Another option is to locate a single bolt anchor on the right, above a dry 8m rap. It's up to you.

Bushwhack up and left to a big fence around a housing estate. Skirt this (keeping an eye out for property developers!) and clamber over a wall to gain the underside of a road bridge.

Getting back to your car isn't as complicated as it looks, although it does require some improvisation. Having crossed the bridge, head directly up the road (Carrer del Mestre Ribera Motes) to join the Banyeres road (CV795) – the road on which you left town before reaching the tunnels. Walk up this for a couple of hundred metres, then turn first right up a small tarmac road with a No Entry sign. Ignoring the next right, go uphill past a few detached houses for several hundred metres until you reach more open country with disused terraces. Just past a walled enclosure and shed on the right, before you get to a second walled enclosure, is a cart track on the right. Follow this track, passing under a ruin on a small hill, and find a way across olive terraces to a rocky rib upon which sit a pair of large electricity pylons. Scramble up the rocky slopes past the pylons until blocked by a wire fence. Follow this uphill (leftwards) until it leads to the road and your parking area (about 1h 20 mins from the bottom of the canyon).

22. Barranco de les Raboses * 1+

Length	300m
Descent	45m
Gear	rope (1 x 15m) or just harness and slings
Season	January to December
Time	about 1h
Maps	Michelin Costa Blanca road map (123 Zoom; 1:130,000)
	CGDE: 821 Alcoy 29-32; 822 Benisa 30-32; 846 Ibi 28-33; 847
	Villajoyosa 29-33 (all 1:50,000)

Recommended for adventure playground enthusiasts, the fast-food, teeny-bop, dinky-toy Raboses is one of the shortest canyons around, yet it boasts the highest density of fixed hardware of any canyon in this book. Nevertheless, it's fully worthwhile for its scrambling and *via ferrata* sections, its bijou qualities, its uniformly good rock, and its roadside accessibility. If you're in the Alcoy region, it's a handy option to round off the day and it is easily combined with Route 21. Competent climbers may prefer to do without a rope, making do with a couple of long slings for direct aid (two points of aid will be needed by most; a grade of Diff/A0 is suggested).

Access point:
about 1hr 30mins
drive from Calpe

Access

From Alcoy, gain the CV795 and head for Banyeres. After about 7km, take a left (CV801 towards Ibi) and follow this road for 8.3km to a right turn at a bridge over a riverbed. Park by the CLR factory. At this point you are almost in the town of Ibi, which can equally easily be accessed from Alicante on the A7. The 'canyon' is visible as the larger of twin gullies cutting into the rugged hillside above. Walk to the bridge and pick up a track leading up left to open hillside at the foot of the left-hand gully. Head diagonally right across the bulging limestone pavement (yellow and white markings) to reach a dry valley and descend to the head of the gorge (20min).

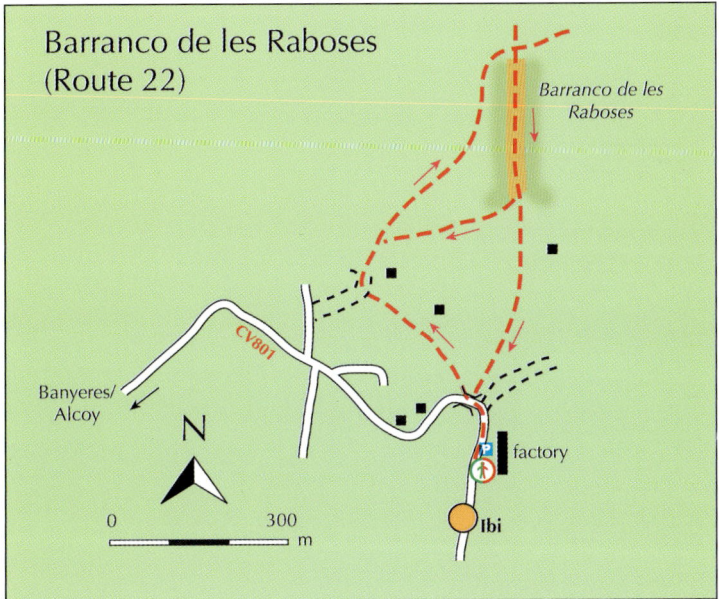

Barranco de les Raboses
(Route 22)

Barranco de les Raboses

CV801

Banyeres/
Alcoy

N

factory

Ibi

0   300
          m

Descent

A few short abseils (<8m) are interspersed between scrambling and *via ferrata* sections. The pitches are short, fully bolted, and fully equipped for down-climbing (or indeed up-climbing should the fancy take you). ▶ When you emerge, either contour across to the approach path or head straight down the riverbed back to your car (1h total).

The canyon features, though miniature in scale, are clean and interesting.

23. Barranco de Relleu ** 2+

Length	800m
Descent	100m
Gear	rope (1 x 50m or 1 x 12m if you down-climb the first section), wetsuit, two vehicles
Season	January to December

Time	3h30, return 15km/40min by car
Maps	Michelin Costa Blanca road map (123 Zoom; 1:130,000)
	CGDE: 821 Alcoy 29-32; 822 Benisa 30-32; 846 Ibi 28-33; 847
	Villajoyosa 29-33 (all 1:50,000)

This remarkably flat-bedded, deep, elongated and inescapable gorge has lots of swimming pools and a remote and unspoilt feel. This is despite a rather unpromising approach, a lowland setting and the presence of a silted-up dam at the start. Best in clean water in spring, or after heavy rain, it can unfortunately get smelly and muddy in a drought. It is possible to hike over the adjacent hills to return to the start, but there is no path and having two cars will save a lot of unpleasant effort.

Access point:
about 40mins drive
from Calpe

Access

Although the gorge is quite short as the crow flies, its start and finish are about 15km apart by road. If you have two cars, leave one at the bottom end, in Orxeta. Orxeta is halfway between Sella and Villajosa on the CV770, with easy access from Finestrat and Benidorm. At the top end of the seasonal lake there is a bridge; at the Sella end there is a huge billboard saying 'Amadorio' 150m and a minor road. Follow this for about 100m and park by another smaller bridge.

To get to the head of the canyon, drive towards Sella on the CV770 and turn left just after the Finestrat/Benidorm junction, signposted Relleu. After 6.5km, bypass Relleu by turning left, soon meeting a junction signposted Pantan de Amadorio SXVIII. Turn left here. Continue for about 3km until greeted by a similar second sign, turn left and go down the dirt road for about 400m until it becomes impassable (good pullout by a solitary pine tree). Gear up and continue on foot for another 400m until you reach a flat meadow. On the left is an old dam, only a few feet high on this side but concealing an impressive gorge on the other. The descent starts here.

There is no escape from the Barranco de Relleu!

Crossing the deep pools in the Barranco de Relleu (credit: the Orange House)

Descent

Over the left-hand end of the dam wall, steps have been hacked into the rock. Competent scramblers will follow these almost to the gorge floor, where a short rap may be necessary next to a fixed cable. Alternatively, abseil in one long pitch from anchors level with the rim of the dam. (This is the only abseil pitch.) From here, an impressive, narrow channel leads twisting and turning through steep cliffs that cut through a ridge of hills. Sometimes it's attractive, sometimes muddy and smelly, depending on the levels of recent rainfall. You'll soon find out which. At its reemergence on the other side of the ridge, follow the widening canyon to the bridge at Orxeta and the welcoming snacks and beers in your support vehicle. Alternatively, contrive a way back to the start by going for a lovely hill walk in your wetsuit – probably best achieved by aiming for the peak on the true left bank.

MALLORCA

The island of Mallorca lies several hundred kilometres off the Spanish mainland, roughly level with Valencia. The Mallorcan canyons are situated in the limestone massif of the Sierra de Tramuntana, which rises above the island's incredibly rugged northern coastline. Most of the canyons have been explored and documented only recently and many of the latest discoveries terminate at remote coastal cliff locations that are not normally accessible. An exception is the well-known and much-travelled Torrente de Pareis, which is probably the easiest as well as the most spectacular canyon in the area, well within the capability of most walkers in the dry season. At the other extreme, Sa Fosca is a long and serious descent that should only be attempted by experienced parties.

Practicalities
Getting there
Low-fare airlines have tended to displace the charter flights that used to dominate the market. British Midland fly daily from Heathrow. British Airways franchisee GB Airways flies daily from Gatwick. Air Europa go from Gatwick Tue/Fri/Sun only. Iberia fly direct from Gatwick (Sat/Sun) and from Heathrow via mainland Spain daily. Easyjet fly daily from Stansted, Luton, Gatwick, Bristol,

The rugged coastline of northern Mallorca, where several canyons emerge directly to sea cliffs (Route 26)

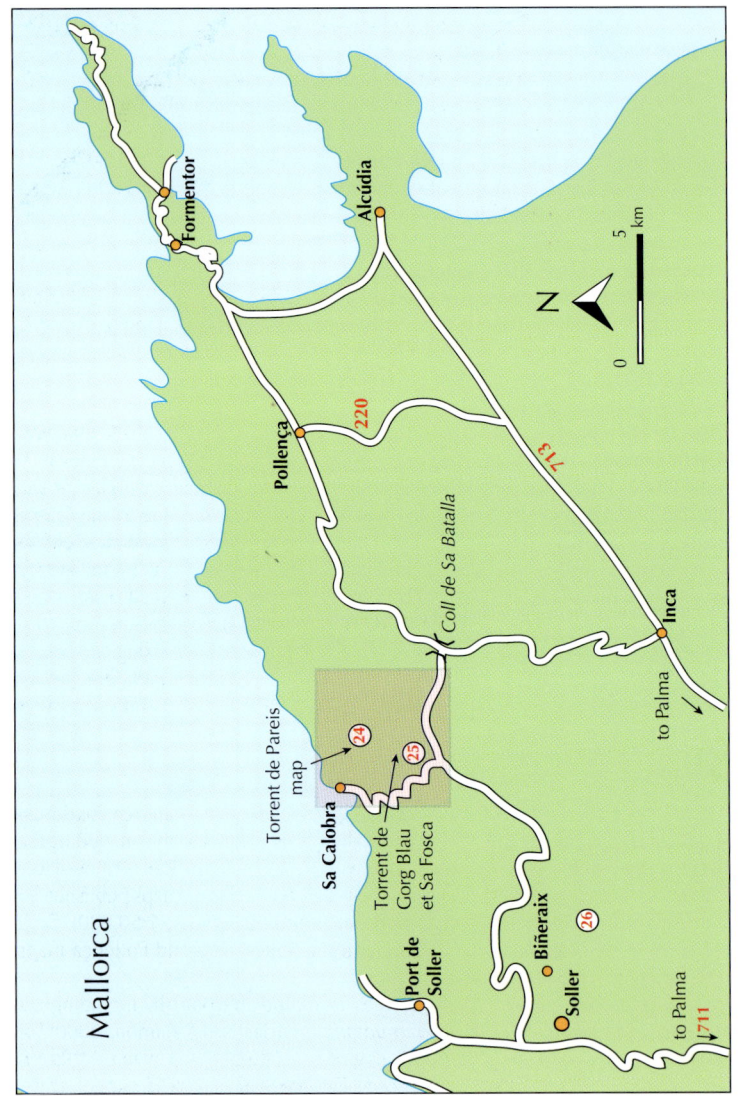

Liverpool, Belfast and Newcastle. Bmibaby fly daily from East Midlands, Cardiff and Manchester. Air Scotland go from Glasgow, Edinburgh and Aberdeen. In addition, there are ferries to Mallorca from Valencia and Barcelona, but they are not cheap. Palma de Mallorca airport (PMI) is located 8km east of Palma (tel: (134) 971 789 000)

For transfer to Palma, most tour operators organise transport. For those that don't, there are several buses that connect the airport to Palma and other major towns and resorts on the island.

When to go
Canyoning is possible all year. Several of the canyons are dry year-round. Others are aquatic in the spring and dry in the summer, by which time the island is becoming rather parched in appearance.

Where to stay and getting around
Most visitors will arrive in Palma and stay in the cheap and plentiful accommodation on the south coast of the island. As the attractions (canyoning and otherwise) are spread around the island, there is no ideal centre. However, with a hire car, any island location can be accessed within 2h, and it is feasible to stay in the package holiday strips on the south coast and make day trips. Many people opt for a package deal that includes a self-catering apartment. Good accommodation is available in Bunyola, close to Sa Gubia (email: honorvell@honorvell.com).

Having said that, the more attractive area of Soller is perhaps the most convenient place for a base, as this area also has some of the best walking and climbing. Soller is accessible by train from Palma, has a connecting tram that goes to the port and a bus service to Pollença that crosses the mountains and is useful for some of the best walks and canyons.

Maps and guides
A good general map for getting around is the GeoCenter Mallorca road map (1:160,000). Several popular tourist and walking maps are available, including the Reise Know-How series of four maps covering the island (Reise Know-How Verlag, 1:40,000). Especially useful are the topographic survey maps published by the military survey organisation (Centro Geográfico del Ejército, 1:50,000). Each sheet covers approximately 27x18km, and the Soller, Inca and Pollença maps cover most of the areas of interest.

There are several canyoning guides available in Spanish, including *Els Torrents Clàssics de la Sierra de Tramuntana* (M Trias and F Ramon, 2000) for Mallorca only, and the more wide-ranging *Asturias, Cuenca, Granada, Mallorca, Tarragona y Terruel, Guia de Descenso de Canobesy Barrancos* (E Gomez and L

MALLORCA ROUTES	Grade	Quality	Rock	Length (km)	Desc (m
24. Torrente de Pareis	1+ 〰	***	L	6.0	18
25. Torrente de Gorg Blau et Sa Fosca	5/6	****	L	6.5	58
26. Other canyons in the Sierra de Tramuntana	3–4	Up to ***	L	-	-
L – limestone					

Tajero, 2004). Try searching for the area you are interested in in the 'Base des Canyons' area of the French website www.descente-canyon.com for more information.

Other activities
Mallorca is the largest island in the Balearic archipelago. Despite the tourist developments that line much of the island's coast, the capital, Palma, retains a historical atmosphere with its narrow streets and Gothic cathedral.

The north-west coast has plenty of secluded coves below the peaks of the Sierra de Tramuntana, and several old towns and villages. The northern coast road is well worth investigating. Enthusiasts of Roman history may be interested to

eason	Time	Gear (optional/seasonal)	Access
ll year	4hr	-	1–2 cars
ll year	8hr–10hr	rope, wetsuit, lamp	1–2 cars
ll year	-	rope (wetsuit)	-

know that Robert Graves, author of the Claudius books, is buried in the local cemetery in the tiny hilltop village of Deia. A drive out to the Formentor peninsula is a mandatory part of many Mallorcan holidays – tour buses are a hassle but the scenery is superb. June Parker's guide *Walking in Mallorca* (Cicerone Press) is a good source of information for walks and scrambles in the Sierra de Tramuntana. There is good scrambling on the Cavall Bernat ridge, accessed from the Boquer valley, near Pollença.

Mallorca is also an established rock-climbing destination, and the quality of the routes and variety of crags that are peppered all over the island is pretty good. The best guide is published by Rockfax. In the north, water sports, including scuba diving are popular, and there is a diving school in Port Sóller.

THE ROUTES

All the canyons are limestone, and some incredible orange rock formations are on display. The Pareis (Route 24) is not to be missed and is suitable as an introduction to canyoning, while the other canyons give much more technical, often aquatic, outings.

24. Torrente de Pareis *** 1+ ≈

Length	6km
Descent	180m
Gear	usually a dry descent, when T-shirt, shorts and trainers are all you need.
Season	January to December
Time	approach 1h30, descent 2h, return 20min plus 20km by road
Maps	CGDE 643/644 Pollença and 671 Inca (both 1:50,000)

This famous gorge gives a very popular outing. The Pareis has cut through huge rock walls, leaving towering cliffs over 300m high, and the scenery is wild and very impressive. After rain, pools may form and the rocks may be slippery and unpleasant. Two cars are useful, although hitching a lift from Sa Calobra is not usually a problem. In summer it is possible to take a bus from Soller to Escorca and return from Sa Calobra to Soller by boat (last boat around 16:45 – check in Soller for details).

Access point:
about 1hr drive from
Palma

Access

Start at the Restaurante Escorca, on the mountain road (C710) between Soller and Pollença. Go through the gates of the small church of Sant Pere and pass it on the right. Some steps lead up left past an old olive tree. From here turn right and follow the farm track to two gates. Take the left-hand one, continuing to a signpost and a big litter bin. Follow a path through woodland, crossing an iron gate. A few minutes later, take a left turn by a

Looking down to the Entreforc from the approach to the Gorge de Pareis

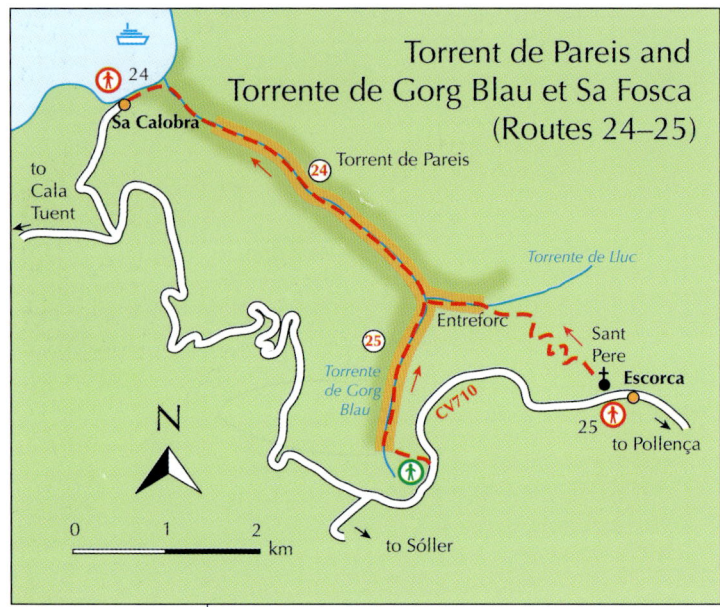

Torrent de Pareis and
Torrente de Gorg Blau et Sa Fosca
(Routes 24–25)

cairn. From here the path is clear and makes a zigzag descent into the gorge – the Torrente de Lluc.

Descent
Once in the streambed turn left and follow the gorge to a junction with a second gorge coming in from the left (Torrente de Gorg Blau). This junction is known as the Entreforc and there is usually a signpost (should it be needed) indicating the way down to Sa Calobra. Red paint marks show the way down the gorge. The difficulties begin after you are about 20min into the gorge proper and are limited to a few scrambling sections. Some route-finding skills are required, especially in the sections of large boulders, but with some exploration an easy way can always be found. Aid is often available from short fixed ropes – some of these are in poor condition, but they do confirm that you are going the right way.

Deep inside Mallorca's amazing Torrente de Pareis

Eventually, you arrive at a huge natural amphitheatre which opens into the sea. The mouth of the Torrente de Pareis is like Piccadilly Circus, and, because few tourists venture far up the canyon, the teeming hordes come as a shock. Go through a tunnel on the left to emerge into the tiny harbour of Sa Calobra. From here, unless you have already left a second vehicle, you should be able to hitch back up to your car without too much trouble.

25. Torrente de Gorg Blau et Sa Fosca **** 5/6

Length	6.5km
Descent	580m
Gear	2 x 30m ropes, full wetsuits (depending on the season and recent weather), headlamps
Season	all year but spring is best for clean aquatic conditions
Time	15min approach, 7h descent, 1h30–2h return to the road (or continue down the Torrente de Pareis – 2h)
Maps	CGDE 643/644 Pollença and 671 Inca (both 1:50,000)

This long and serious route is, for some of its length, a caving exercise. It takes the canyon that joins the Torrente de Lluc at the Entreforc above the Torrente de Parais (Route 24). Highly rated for its variety of formations, the gorge is very atmospheric and is considered to be one of the best in Europe. It is best done in spring when aquatic conditions are optimal. At other times, the volume of water flowing can depend on the recent weather as well as hydroelectric activity at the feeder reservoir above. If water is flowing it will be cold whatever the time of year; if not the pools can be putrid especially in summer.

Access point: about 1hr drive from Palma

Access
The gorge can be reached in 15min from the Central Electrica building on the Soller–Pollença road (C710). There are two alternative starts that lead to the climactic

Impressive aloe vegetation at the Entreforc in the Torrente de Pareis

lower section, Sa Fosca, which is so deep that you will be in complete darkness through a section of 400m, which normally takes about 2h to negotiate. It is possible to escape from the gorge before this section. Should you choose to make the descent to the Entreforc, you have the choice of descending the Pareis (see Route 24) or hiking uphill to join the C710 at the church of Sant Pierre. Either way makes a fantastic outing.

26. Other canyons in the Sierra de Tramuntana

Here are a few tips if you want to branch out into the newly developed canyons of the Tramuntana.

Torrente de Biñeraix *** 4

Time	4–5h (approach 1h15, descent 2h30, return 45mins)
Gear	full wetsuit (depending on season and recent weather), 2 x 45m ropes

Accessed by a lovely approach walk from Biniaraix, 1km west of Soller, this is a fine descent with several waterfalls. Park between Biniaraix and S'estret. Follow the path uphill towards the gorge, crossing the watercourse a couple of times before skirting the main canyon on its north side. Drop down into the gorge, where a series of about 13 abseils (6–30m) lead you back to the approach path. The **Torrente de l'Offre** is located hereabouts near the village of the same name.

Torrente de s'Esmolar ** 3

Time	3h
Gear	2 x 45m ropes

Almost always dry, this canyon is a tributary of the Torrente de Lluc. It can be reached in 20 minutes from Esorca on the Soller–Pollença road (C710).Descent takes about 3h.

Torrente de Mortitx ** 4

Length	500m
Descent	100m
Time	6–7h (approach 1h15; descent 2h; return 3h30)
Gear	1 x 45m rope, spare ropes for fixing, jumars or equivalent

Access, which is from the village of Mortitx on the Soller–Pollença road (C710), is tricky and a local guide-book will be needed. A classic initial section leads to difficult route-finding and an atmospheric finale amid sea cliffs. Calm seas required. Especially suited to cavers as you have to climb fixed ropes (condition variable) to reverse the route.

Torrente de Coanegra/Torrente del Frau ** 3

Time	3–4h (approach 15min, descent 2h, return 1h)
Gear	wetsuit, 1 x 40m rope

A good canyon that is best done after a wet spell to avoid smelly pools.

Other canyons in the Sierra de Tramuntana have been explored, including **Cova Negra 3** (total time 5h), **Guix 3** (total time 4–5h), **Almadrá 3** (total time 4–5h), **Na Mora 3+** (a canyon of 1.5km length and 120m descent, 30m rope required) and the **Gorg de Diners 4** (total time 7–8h).

FRANCE

*Tell me who will keep score for you
As we play every day inside a deep karma canyon.
Maybe you can turn the karma into happy ever after.
If you find a way to do this, I'd appreciate a hand, I'm in a deep karma canyon.*

Bob Mould, 'Deep Karma Canyon'

In France, canyoning has been a mainstream activity for some years and descents are a regular feature of the year for many enthusiasts. As the national psyche is attuned to the convenience of ski-tows and fully bolted rock-climbs, it comes as no surprise to find that canyons are equally exploited as an outdoor resource, with all the guide services and commercialisation this implies. You will find few tatty abseil stations here.

In August, when seemingly the whole of France decamps *en masse* to the holiday regions (either the sun-and-sand or the sun-and-hills depending on their disposition), some areas can get crowded. Luckily, French canyons are an almost infinite resource. Some of the best are in Haute-Provence, the area that encompasses the Verdon Gorge. The canyons are as varied as the region itself, and range from the gentle, easy-going gradients of the Gorges d'Opodette in the Luberon to the huge impressive chasms of the Verdon and its tributaries such as the Artuby and Mainmorte. Some canyons are descended regularly in the high season, and, while the crowds may detract from your experience, the state of fixed gear is generally very high as a result. In any case, the wealth of canyoning possibilities means that it is always possible to escape the crowds, and, except in the Verdon itself, you are unlikely to meet anybody at all. Make sure you go. It's spectacular.

Along the coast in the Mercantour-Nice region there are numerous other possibilities. Also, the island of Corsica has some canyons of high repute (further information in Appendix 2), as does the pre-Pyrenean area around Céret to the south of Perpignan. Coverage of these areas will have to wait for a future edition of this guide.

HAUTE-PROVENCE

Haute-Provence is within a wedge of territory defined by Apt and Sisteron in the west of the region, and the Verdon and Castellane in the east. The area is large and

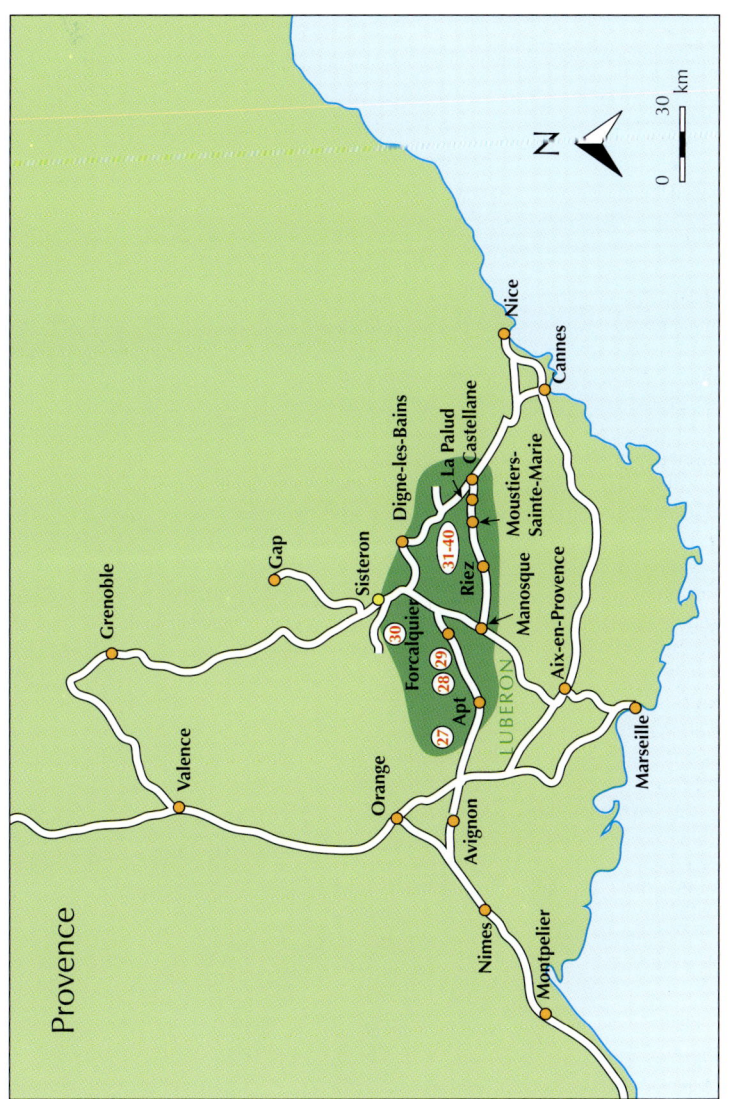

Provence

Nice

Cannes

Digne-les-Bains

La Palud
Castellane

Moustiers-
Sainte-Marie

Gap

Sisteron

31–40

Riez

Manosque

Aix-en-Provence

Grenoble

30

Forcalquier

29

28

Apt

27

LUBERON

Valence

Orange

Avignon

Marseille

Nîmes

Montpelier

N

0   30   km

Between two canyons – the unique setting of Moustiers, Haute-Provence

highly diverse, and, unlike the Sierra de Guara in the Spanish Pyrenees, there is no clear-cut centre of canyoning activity. The area is popular with climbers and walkers in the spring and autumn seasons, although all the canyons described can also be descended in summer. In fact there is no clear season for canyoning, as many of the canyons are dry except after heavy rain, while others are too dangerous to descend in such circumstances and are best left to drier periods. Therefore you can choose dry or wet descents according to your inclination (and whether you have a wetsuit) almost throughout the season.

There are several guiding outfits, especially in the Verdon area, that offer canyoning alongside climbing and other activities and each has its pet canyons on offer. Guiding services and equipment hire possibilities can be found in Moustiers-Ste-Marie, Castellane, and La Palud-sur-Verdon. Most of the local canyoning companies are listed in the Verdon/Activities/Canyoning area of the Provence Web website (www.provenceweb.fr). In Moustiers, the guide shop down the hill from the main square should be able to help out (www.verdon-passion.com, closed lunchtimes). In La Palud, the Bureau des Guides is open every day from 09:00–12:00 and 16:30–19:30 in July and August; and from 10:00–12:00 and 16:30–18:30 at weekends and holidays in September to June (tel: (+33) 492 773 050, www.escalade-verdon.com).

The selection in this chapter covers only the southern section of Haute-Provence and the canyoning trips chosen range in scale from an hour or two to a full day. There are further canyoning opportunities in the north of the region around Barcellonette, where the river Ubaye passes through on its way to join the Durance, and around Allos and Colmars, close to where the Verdon has its origin.

Practicalities
Getting there
The central town in Haute-Provence is Digne les Bains, roughly equidistant (about 160km) from Nice and Marseille and about 180km south of Grenoble. All three of these gateway cities are served by budget airlines and have good transport links. The simplest way to get to the area is to fly to Marseille, rent a car and make the 2hr drive via Aix-en-Provence. The Apt/Vaucluse area (Routes 27–29) is closer to Marseille than the other canyons, which are in Haute-Provence proper.

British Airways fly from Gatwick to Marseille and Toulon and to Nice from Gatwick, Heathrow and Manchester. Bmibaby fly to Nice from East Midlands. EasyJet fly to Marseille from Gatwick and Liverpool and to Nice from Bristol, Liverpool, Gatwick, Luton and Stansted. GB Airways fly to Toulon and Corsica from Gatwick. Jet2 fly from Leeds Bradford; and Air France flies from Heathrow. Thomsonfly go to Nice and Marseille from Coventry. There are frequent TGV trains from Paris Gare de Lyon to Avignon and there are TGVs from Paris to Marseille and Aix-en-Provence.

From Marseille it is half an hour by train to Avignon. There is also a rail line heading north from Marseille that goes to the Durance valley towns of Manosque and Sisteron, from where you can take buses or hitch hike.

When to go

The main season extends from May to November (**the descent of wet canyons is not permitted outside these months**), although several of the canyons are year-round possibilities. More than other areas in this guide, special attention should be given to recent rainfall, as some gorges (notably the Artuby) can become impassable in spate and others become very serious propositions. On the other hand, many of the easier canyons are at their best after a day or two of rain. In the winter months, much depends on your enthusiasm for cold water, limited daylight and the gloom of a shadowy defile. A few of the canyons have official restrictions on party size and times of day. (These and other details are given in the route descriptions where applicable.) As elsewhere, July and August are good but the canyons can be busy (especially in August) and approach walks can be arduous in the heat, while May, June and September are pleasant and relatively quiet. Restrictions apply in some of the canyons, but small groups are unlikely to be affected (see www.provenceweb.fr for details and updates).

Where to stay

Good, inexpensive campsites are available at Castellane and Moustiers-Ste-Marie, where there are supermarkets, banks and post facilities. These towns are good bases for the Verdon area. Digne is of little interest and does not make a good base. La Palud-sur-Verdon is a small village just a few kilometres from the Verdon Gorge itself, and is a good base for a few days, although it has only a basic supermarket. It has a couple of campsites that are both closed by the end of September when the nights are getting chilly. However, there are several *gîtes* that stay open much longer and are only slightly more expensive. In the west of the area, there are decent municipal campsites at Apt and Bonnieux, which may be of interest to climbers destined for Buoux and the other low-altitude Provence crags and for walkers and cyclists exploring the Luberon.

Getting around

For most of the canyons you will need your own transport. Moustiers-Ste-Marie, from which you can walk to several canyons, is a good base for those without a vehicle. Around La Palud, Point Sublime and the Verdon, one-way walks are so common that several taxi and minibus operators cater specifically for walkers.

The amazing Verdon Gorge

There is a taxi rank in La Palud or taxis can be booked (tel: 06 07 65 19 49). Taxi Verdon (tel: 06 68 18 13 13) are prompt, friendly and reliable. Hitching is a real possibility, although traffic can be sparse on the Verdon's north rim loop road and there is a one-way section in the middle of the loop.

Maps and guides

The Michelin road map 245 Provence Côte d'Azur (1:200,000), available every-where, is incredibly detailed and will get you to the canyon areas (and to most of the canyons) in conjunction with this book. Consider buying the Michelin motor-ing atlas, which covers the whole of France at the same scale – it may work out cheaper if you are travelling around.

For footpaths, contours and other useful detail, you will need the appropri-ate Institute Géographique National (IGN) map: the Carte de Randonée series is exemplary. The relevant IGN maps are 31420T and 32420T in the Apt region, and the 33410T for the Sisteron area. For the Verdon area, IGN map 34420T is indispensable and covers all but one of the canyons described. For the canyons themselves, further detail can be found in the Edisud guide *Descente de canyons dans les Alpes de Haute-Provence* by (B Gorgeon, E Olive and P

HAUTE-PROVENCE ROUTES	Grade	Quality	Rock	Length (km)	Des (r
27. Gorges de Véroncle	2	*	L	3.5	10
28. Gorges d'Opodette	2	**	L	2.5	6
29. Grand Vallot d'Opodette	2		L	1.0	1
30. Gorges du Valbelle	3	**	L	5.0	3
31. Ravin du Balène	2+	*	L	0.5	5
32. Ravin de Riou	3	***	L	1.5	2
33. Ravin de Notre Dame	2	**	L	1.5	1
34. Ravin de Vénascle	3 ⌇	***	L	2.5	2
35. Ravin d'Angouire	3 ⌇	***	L	4.0	3
36. Verdon Gorge – upper section	1	****	L	10.0	4 tot
37. Verdon Gorge – middle section	2	***	L	8.0	5
38. Verdon Gorge side-canyons:					
Mainmorte	4–5	***	L	1.5	70
Font de Barbin	4–5	**	L	1.5	9
Ferne	4–5	**	L	0.5	70
Cabrielle	4–5	**	L	0.5	75
39. Le Baou	3 ⌇	**	L	9.0	2
40. L'Artuby	3 ⌇	***	L	4.0	5
	3-	***	L	2.5	46

ª – Restrictions usually apply outside these months; L – limestone

Tordjman, 2006), *Canyons de Haute-Provence* (J-F Fiorina, F Jourdan and P Tordjman, 2006). For the Verdon (middle section), side-canyons, and Artuby (Routes 37, 38 and 40), you should check water levels (tel: (+33) 492 826 268) before you go.

Other activities

Provence is so large and diverse that all manner of outdoor activities are catered for. There are many walks in the Vaucluse, Luberon and Verdon areas and climbers are spoilt for choice on the perfect limestone of the famous crags of Verdon, Buoux and many others. Virtually every village has a museum and a church that are worth a visit and the larger towns invariably have interesting markets on top of the usual hustle and bustle. Tourist information offices in Moustiers-Ste-Marie and La Palud (in the town hall 'Le Château', 04120 La Palud-sur-Verdon; tel: 04 92 77

eason	Time	Gear (optional/seasonal)	Access
year	3hr45–4hr45	(rope)	car
r–Nov[a]	2hr15	rope (wetsuit)	car
year	1hr	rope (wetsuit)	car
ay–Nov[a]	4hr30–5hr30	rope (wetsuit)	1–2 cars
ay–Nov	2hr	rope (wetsuit)	car or taxi from Moustiers
ay–Oct[a]	5hr30	rope (wetsuit)	walk from Moustiers
year	3hr	rope (wetsuit)	walk from Moustiers
year	6hr	rope (wetsuit)	car or taxi from Moustiers
ay–Nov[a]	5hr45	rope (wetsuit)	car or taxi from Moustiers
year	5hr–6hr	torch	car + taxi or 2 taxis from La Palud
year	5hr–8hr	wetsuit	car + taxi or 2 taxis from La Palud
year	8hr	rope, wetsuit	1–2 cars
est May–Sept)	9hr		or 2 taxis
	5hr15		from La
	5hr		Palud
ay–Nov[a]	5hr20	rope, wetsuit	car + taxi or 2 taxis from La Palud
ay–Oct	6hr	wetsuit	car
year	7hr	rope	car

137

32 02, www.lapaludsurverdon.com) are useful sources of information for the Verdon area and give away free leaflets in English covering local walking routes.

White water rafting and canoeing are popular in the Verdon. For white water guiding and equipment, useful information can be found on the Provence Web website www.provenceweb.fr. Local companies include: Aboard Rafting, BP19–8, Place de l'Eglise, 04120 Castellane, tel/fax: 04 92 83 76 11, email: info@aboard-rafting.com; and Nathalie et Pascal Faudou, 04120 La Palud sur Verdon, tel/fax: 04 92 77 30 43, email: info@aventuresetnature.com.

For a lazy day, rent a pedalo on the Lac de Saint Croix, from where you can venture up the lower reaches of the Verdon gorge (if you don't mind being amid a flotilla of similar craft). The drive around the Verdon Gorge is well worthwhile for spectacular views – don't forget your camera. Aim to finish on the northern rim's roadside belvederes at dusk, where huge vultures glide silently past you on the evening thermals, only a few metres from the cliff edge.

Further afield, cities such as Aix-en-Provence and Avignon are within a day trip from Apt and the Luberon and have plenty of galleries, cinemas and other places of interest for those occasional rainy days. Roman and Medieval buildings abound in the southern part of the region. And, as ever in Provence, it is easy to while away the hours over a beer at a simple café or over a relaxed meal at any manner of restaurant, wherever you happen to find yourself.

THE ROUTES

All the canyons covered here are limestone, ranging in scale from the modest to the gargantuan, from short 'n' easy to long 'n' scary (see Appendix 5).

Access to wet canyons in the Alpes de Haute-Provence (including Routes 30 and 32 if water is flowing) is restricted to between 10:00 and 18:00 by the regional authorities .

Apt and the Vaucluse area

Vaucluse is really an area distinct from Haute-Provence. The canyons in this area are relatively humble, in no way comparable with the stately gorges of Verdon. However, they are not without charm, and, while not being especially worthwhile objectives for a canyoning trip in themselves, are perfectly good targets if you happen to be in the area. If your fingers are trashed from pocket-pulling at Buoux, your legs destroyed from pedalling up Mont Ventoux or you have blisters from hiking in the Luberon, they form worthy little expeditions suitable for beginners (especially Route 27). On a wet day, they would make a pleasant change from sitting in Apt waiting for the sun to come out.

*27. Gorges de Véroncle * 2*

Length	3.5km
Descent	about 100m
Gear	rope (1 x 30m, optional)
Season	January to December
Time	approach 1h30–2h, descent 2–2h30, return 10min
Maps	Michelin road map 245 (1:200,000)
	Institut Géographique National (IGN): 31420T and 32420T

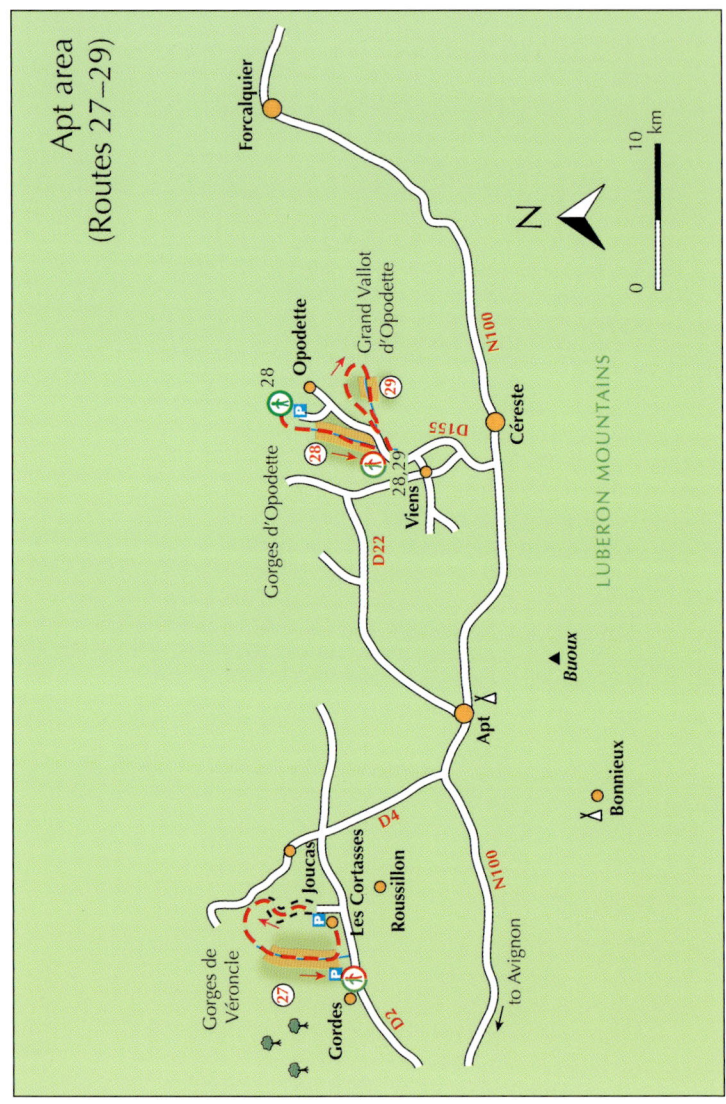

Apt area
(Routes 27–29)

This gorge is suited to a leisurely approach and is popular with walkers (usually going uphill!). Following an earthquake in 1887 the gorge became essentially dry, a calamity that put paid to the local water mills, the remains of which are still in evidence. For those wishing to travel light or avoid any technical sections, the path poses few problems and the gorge can be approached as a simple gorge walk, in which case T-shirt, shorts and trainers are perfectly adequate. However, some running water or pools may be encountered in the lower reaches, where the path avoids the bottom of the gorge. If desired, the steep sections in this part of the gorge can be descended by abseil, although all difficulties can be avoided by easy walking. In either case, the gorge is ideal for beginners.

Catch the flue in the Gorges de Véroncle

Approach

From Apt, the gorge is about a 17km drive. Take the N100 towards Avignon for about 5km, then turn right on the D4. After 6.5km take a left, and head towards Gordes for about 4km, looking out for a sign to Les Cortasses on the right. Ignore this, but continue towards Gordes for a few hundred metres, turning right (easily missed) to limited parking at the foot of the wooded slopes above.

The gorge is hidden in these woods, and here you have a choice depending on whether you want to (a) walk up through the woods and make a circular loop back into the gorge (recommended) or (b) walk up the gorge itself. For (a), make your way across the river and continue back to Les Cortasses on paths that come and go (some private land, so improvisation may be required), turn left and go through the village to woodland (1km; you can also park here), where a rough gravel road continues uphill. Walk up the gravel road through the woods, passing a refuge (open in summer) after about 1h. Continue up a metalled road to Murs, or, better if time is pressing, take paths on the left and drop down into the gorge, the start of which is marked by a stone bridge (1h30–2h). For (b), simply follow the way-marked footpath (yellow at first, then blue) up the gorge itself.

Descent

The upper part of the gorge is a simple stroll, characterised by dense woodland through which the path winds a peaceful way. The first landmark is a ruined mill, the Moulin des Étangs (at about 410m), where you have the entertaining option of descending a steep flue in the remains of the building (rope usually *in situ*). As you continue walking, the gorge gradually narrows and you encounter several more ruined mills. After about 45min, the path skirts a steep section by ascending to the gorge rim on the right. For the purist wanting a descent of the narrows, abseil chains are in place, allowing a direct descent (15m pitch plus an optional smaller pitch, and a

The avoidable narrows in the Gorges de Véroncle

pool that can be very smelly). Continue down the streambed in a narrow section between high gorge walls. Interest is maintained to the bottom of the gorge, where you have the option of descending rock steps or ladders or abseiling the true line (five or six pitches of 5–10m, all fully equipped). Soon after the gorge opens out you will reach the valley and your car.

28. Gorges d'Opodette ** 2

Length	2.5km
Descent	60m
Gear	20m rope, wetsuit (optional)
Season	April to November
Time	approach 10min, descent 1h30, return 30min
Maps	IGN Pierrevert–Reillane 3242 Est; Banon 3241 Est, 1:25000

This is a mostly dry canyon with some deep pools that can be quickly waded. It gives a pleasant trip through a typically modest Vaucluse canyon.

Access point:
about 25km from Apt

Approach
From Apt, head east on the N100 for 15km and turn left (north) to follow the winding road towards the tiny hamlet of Opodette (10km). Just before Opodette, take a small road into the trees on the left to a rough parking area (signposted). The gorge is at your feet.

Descent
Follow a winding path from the parking area to the bottom of the gorge. Easy walking leads down the gorge, which runs in southerly direction full on into the midday sun. After about 1.5km, the gorge narrows and a series of potholes must be negotiated. These are usually about 1–2m deep in water, and are followed by a short pitch (4–5m, chains, rope sometimes in place). Continue for a further kilometre to reach a junction with the Grand

Dry canyon, wet pools – Gorges d'Opodette

Vallot on the left and a bridge that you drove over earlier. A steep scramble leads up left to the road. To get back to your vehicle, follow the road uphill for 30min. Alternatively, complete your trip with a detour to the Grand Vallot (Route 29).

29. Grand Vallot d'Opodette 2

Length	1km
Descent	110m
Gear	30m rope, wetsuit (optional)
Season	all year
Time	approach 20min, descent 1h, return 5min
Maps	IGN Pierrevert–Reillane 3242 Est and Banon 3241 Est, 1:25000

This short tributary of the Calavon (the seasonal river that occupies the Gorge d'Opodette) is hardly worthwhile on its own but can be combined with the Gorge d'Opodette to round off the day. Like that gorge, it is essentially bereft of running water, although a few bracing dips in static pools are likely to be encountered. A wetsuit is recommended, at least outside the height of summer. It is a canyon in miniature.

Access point:
about 25km from Apt

Approach
As for the Gorges d'Opodette, from Apt head east on the N100 for 15km and turn left (north) to follow the winding road towards the tiny hamlet of Opodette. Park near the bridge about 2km short of the hamlet and walk uphill for a couple of minutes to a dirt road leading off to the right. Follow this, then a vague path that skirts the small cliff at the mouth of the gorge on its left (as you look at it). Scrub then gives way to a field. Skirt this, cross a small stream and wooded area to another field and work down right to reach a streambed where it steps down into a steep little defile.

The tiny initial abseil pitch of the Grand Vallot d'Opodette

Descent

Technicalities start immediately with a very short abseil pitch (a single bolt right at the start is hard to spot but a chain can be found slightly downstream on the right bank). Several waist-deep pools are encountered before a couple of more substantial pitches lead to a junction with the approach path. Ignore this, and continue down the streambed past another short pitch to join the main Gorge d'Opodette under its bridge, from where a short scramble leads to the road and your car.

Sisteron area

This isolated canyon (Route 30) is very close to the town and crags of Sisteron and is well worth doing if you're passing through or based in the area. It cuts through rugged, forested terrain and almost has a mountain atmosphere.

30. Gorges du Valbelle ** 3

Length	5km
Descent	350m
Gear	30m rope, wetsuit
Season	May to November (descents are restricted to these months, between 10:00–18:00)
Time	approach 10min, descent 3–4h, return 1h
Map	IGN Ribiers–Montagnes de Lure 3340 Ouest, 1:25000

This inescapable ravine gives a committing yet fun descent. Pools and dead water in summer give way to exciting water flow and noisy falls after rainy spells.

Approach

From Sisteron, head south on the N85 for 3km, turn left for Noyers (D964) and turn off this road to the left after 7km for Valbelle. Having two cars is ideal, in which case leave one here. With one car, continue for about 10km past the Ferme de Ponchette to a parking area amid the forest on the right. At this point there is a large signboard with an angled roof, and a signpost detailing various paths. From Apt, a winding route can be taken through Forcalquier over the Montaigne de Lure ridge to this point.

Access point:
about 20km from Sisteron

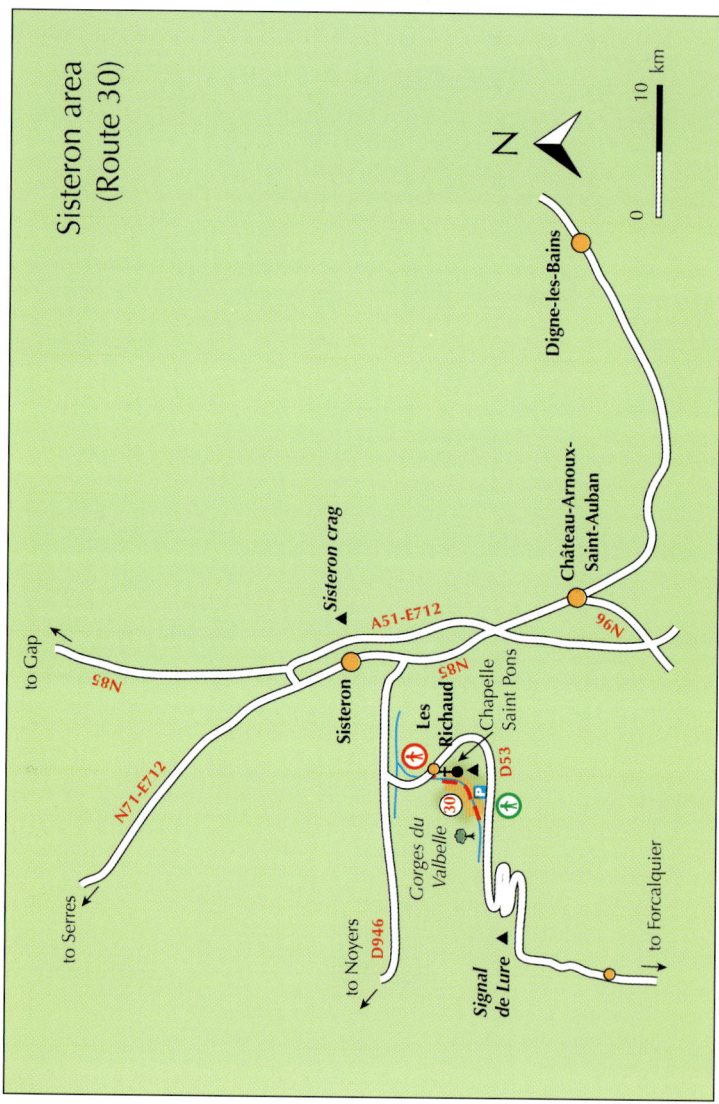

Sisteron area
(Route 30)

Descent

Take the path descending from the car park into the forest, and trend right to pick up the streambed (15min).

Halfway down the Gorges du Valbelle in spate

Walking and scrambling lead down the ravine, which can be noisy and exciting in wet periods. There are seven to eight abseil pitches, fully equipped, interspersed with scrambling and walking sections. One or two of the pitches can be avoided by scrambling, though take care of the rocks which can be very slippery in the wet. ◄

The canyon is a good length, and concentration can become difficult if you start to tire.

At the foot of all difficulties, the terrain levels out and a path leads rightwards from the stream to Les Richaud. If you are lucky, you'll be able to hitch a lift back up to your vehicle, although traffic is sparse. If not, follow the road or a shorter alternative takes a path through the forest, skirting around the back of the limestone peak to the gorge's right (a detour can be made to the hermitage of Chapelle Saint Pons perched high above the gorge), to the parking area.

Moustiers-Ste-Marie area

The unique cliff setting of Moustiers, with the Ravins de Riou (left) and Notre Dame (right)

Moustiers has a unique setting at the foot of a steep band of cliffs. As you approach on the D952 from Riez, the village suddenly comes into view with its dramatic backdrop of Provençal limestone, split on the left by the Ravin de Riou (Route 30) and on the right by the Ravin de Notre Dame (Route 31). As a base, Moustiers is distinctly warmer than La Palud, lying at a lower altitude.

The canyons hereabouts are of a reasonable stature without being hugely impressive, and, while all are worthwhile, the Riou is probably considered the most classic.

31. Ravin de Balène * 2+

Length	0.5km
Descent	50m
Gear	rope (30m), half wetsuit (optional)
Season	May to November
Time	approach 10min, descent 1h30, return 20min

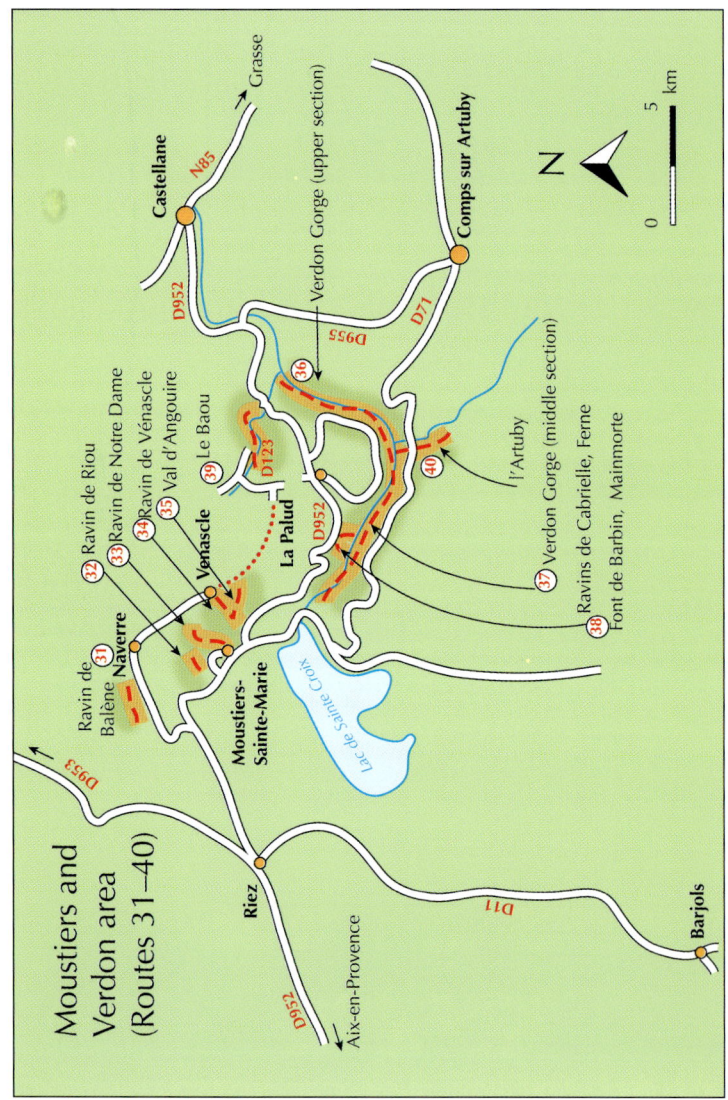

Moustiers and
Verdon area
(Routes 31–40)

Maps	IGN Moustiers-Ste-Marie 3442 Ouest, 1:25,000. Just to access the gorge, the 3441 map (Gorges de Verdon, Moustiers-Ste-Marie) is adequate.

A rather gloomy and slippery canyon that has its share of smelly pools if it has not rained in a while. However, it has some good rock features, gets the midday sun and is usually equipped with fixed ropes for Tyrolean traverses. Access is currently restricted to between 10:00 and 18:00 (see the Canyoning in the Verdon section of the Provence Web website – www.provenceweb.fr – for updates).

Ravin de Balène
(Route 31)

Access point:
about 8km from
Moustiers

Approach

From Moustiers-Ste-Marie, take the D952 towards Riez, but leave it after about 4km (past the hairpins) and turn right towards Naverre and Venascle. After 4km, by a tree with signs for Saint Jurs and Gîte Vauvenière, a gravel road heads down to the left. You can park here, or, better, drive down the gravel road and up the other side for 200–300m to a layby on the left.

Descent

**Be sure to take a
rope for the longer
pitches where in situ
gear may be badly
decayed or missing.**

Head down to the streambed (taking a path on the left before the layby) and follow it pleasantly for a few hundred metres until it narrows and steepens. Most of the pitches are very short and have fixed, knotted ropes for hand-over-handing, but not all. ◄ There are several short Tyroleans over deep pools, and interest is sustained until the gorge ends abruptly in an open glade. A rough path heads up and right to gain the gravel road. Follow this back to your parking place.

32. Ravin de Riou *** 3

Length	1.5km
Descent	240m
Gear	2 x 50m rope, wetsuit
Season	May to October
Time	approach 1h15, descent 4h, return 15min
Map	IGN Gorges de Verdon–Moustiers-Ste-Marie 3442, 1:25,000

A classic descent with a couple of long abseils in impressive scenery. Access restrictions apply (no more than five teams of ten a day), but prior permission not necessery.

Access point:
Moustiers

Approach

From Moustiers-Ste-Marie, at the top of the village's zigzag parking and access road that rises up the hillside towards

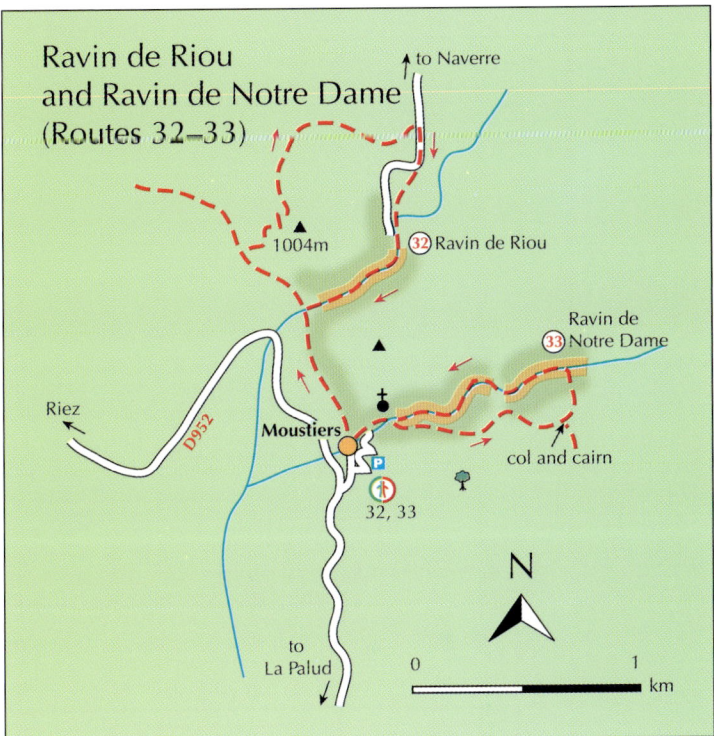

Ravin de Riou
and Ravin de Notre Dame
(Routes 32–33)

to Naverre

▲ 1004m

32 Ravin de Riou

Ravin de
33 Notre Dame

Riez

D952

Moustiers

col and cairn

32, 33

to
La Palud

N

0   1
km

the stone staircase leading to Notre Dame de Beauvoir,
take the yellow-marked path that works its way under the
crags above the village and crosses below the Ravin.
Shortly after meeting woodland, take a right fork and
climb steeply up the hillside, round the flank of the hill,
over a col and along a valley to join a road coming down
from Naverre. Follow this down to the Ravin de Riou.

Descent
A narrow, flat section leads to several short pitches and
pools, then another level section. Suddenly you are into
a series of pitches – two of 15m leading to a pool, then

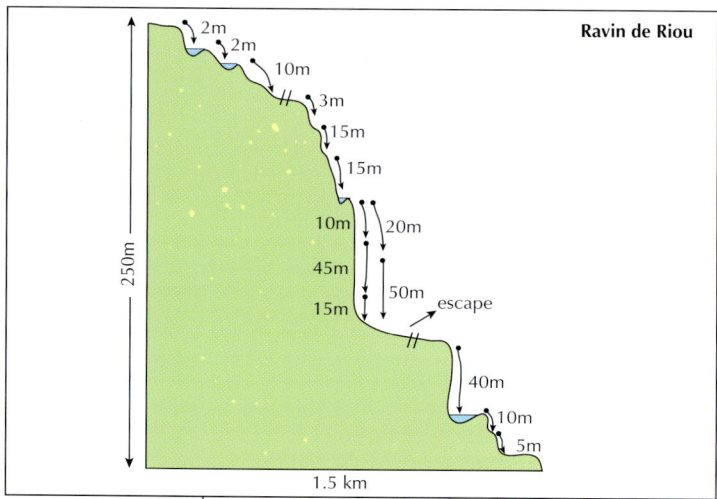

Ravin de Riou

250m

2m
2m
10m
3m
15m
15m
10m
20m
45m
50m escape
15m
40m
10m
5m

1.5 km

one of 20m followed immediately by a long, 50m pitch. One further substantial abseil (40m) is followed by shorter pitches and the gorge exit and an easy walk to the village and your parking place.

*33. Ravin de Notre Dame ** 2*

Length	1.5km
Descent	170m
Gear	25m rope, wetsuit (optional)
Season	January to December
Time	approach 45min, descent 2h, return 15min
Map	IGN Gorges de Verdon–Moustiers-Ste-Marie 3442, 1:25,000

A gorge in two halves: narrow, constricted and tortuous at first, followed by a more open gorge-walking finish. Usually dry, although a small stream makes the upper section interesting after rain.

The steep final section of the Ravin de Riou (Route 32)

One of several small falls in the narrows of the Ravin de Notre Dame

Approach

As for the Ravin de Riou, start at the top of Moustiers-Ste-Marie's parking and access road that rises up the hillside to the east of the village. Take the path and stone staircase leading to the Notre Dame de Beauvoir, but leave it just before reaching the chapel. Cross the streambed and follow the path up the side of the gorge (yellow waymarks). After about 40min, a small ridge is reached. The upper part of the Ravin de Notre Dame lies down to the left, while the main path veers off to the right towards Vincel. Follow a path down to a small side-canyon, and arrive in the main gorge atop a small entry pitch.

Descent

Make a short abseil from the collection of rope slings, or down-climb down to the left. Continue down the excellent, narrow, winding channel through lots of (mostly) shallow pools, making six or seven short rappels (maximum 7m, bolt anchors *in situ*). Suddenly, as you pass a curious cross-stratum of steep limestone, the character of the gorge changes completely as it opens out and a pleasant streambed is followed by mostly easy walking. There are some slabby pitches of 10–15m but these can be avoided by entertaining scrambling usually on the right bank. The gorge curves around to emerge at the chapel and an easy 5min walk back to Moustiers and your car.

Access point:
Moustiers

34. Ravin de Vénascle *** 3 〰

Length	2.5km
Descent	250m
Gear	rope (1 x 40m), wetsuit (depending on recent rainfall)
Map	IGN Gorges de Verdon–Moustiers-Ste-Marie 3442, 1:25,000
Season	April to November preferred, but possible year-round.
Time	approach 1h45, descent 4h, return 15min

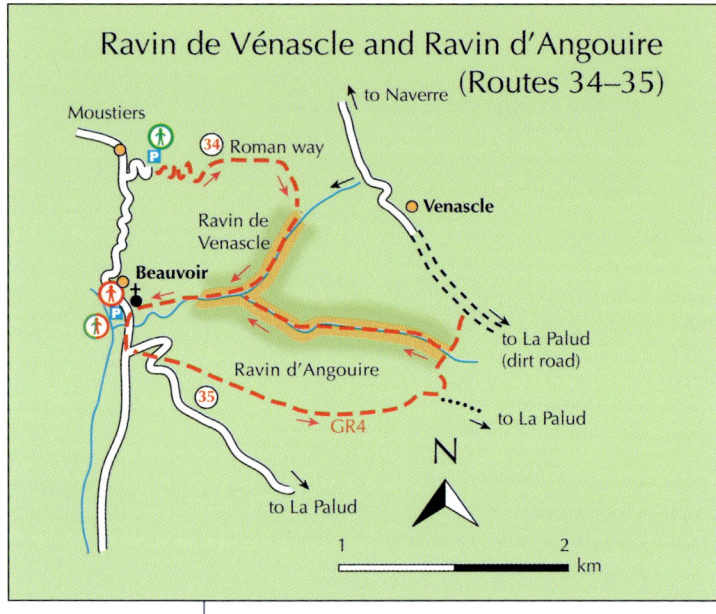

Ravin de Vénascle and Ravin d'Angouire (Routes 34–35)

This is an excellent, long canyon that is usually dry.

Access point:
Moustiers

Approach

Leave your car at the zigzag parking road forming the approach to Moustiers and locate a signposted footpath leading to Venascle on a Roman road leading past the Chapelle Ste Anne. Slog up the Roman way that leads up through the crags to the plateau, where it levels out and leads after about 2km, via a right fork, to the gorge (the left fork leads to the hamlet of Venascle). An **alternative** approach is to drive or take a taxi round from Moustiers (past the approach to the Ravin de Balene, ignoring the gravel road at the tree) and continue for 8km to Venascle and the end of the tarmac road. The humble beginnings of the gorge are on your right.

Descent

A level approach along the streambed leads to narrows and the first of several short abseil pitches and the more open central section of the gorge where escape is possible up either bank. Scrambling leads onward to the lower section, where a series of slightly longer (10–12m) pitches, interspersed with rock scrambles, lead to a junction with the Angouire. Shortly after this, the gorge opens out into wooded slopes, and a path, then road, can be located on the right leading down to Beauvoir and the Chappelle St Pierre. From here a short walk along the road takes you back to Moustiers.

Modest beginnings for the Ravin de Vénascle

163

35. Ravin d'Angouire *** 3 〰

Length	4km
Descent	300m
Gear	rope (1 x 40m), wetsuit
Season	May to November.
Time	approach 1h30, descent 4h, return 15min
Map	IGN Gorges de Verdon–Moustiers-Ste-Marie 3442, 1:25,000

A fine, committing expedition that is usually dry but has many pools and some substantial pitches.

The GR4 meets a Roman road above the Ravin d'Angouire

Approach

Access point: about 5km from Moustiers

Take the D952, heading south out of Moustiers-Ste-Marie, and park in Beauvoir/Chappelle St Pierre. Walk further along the D952 and turn left at the roundabout for La Palud-sur-Verdon. Pick up the GR4 footpath and follow it steeply uphill through woodland to the cliffs above. The path eventually emerges onto the cliff tops and the Plateau de L'Ourbes. After a couple of hundred metres, take a left fork and contour through woodland for about 1.5km to a ruin. Take a left fork, and work down to the bed of the valley.

Alternatively, drive or take a taxi round from Moustiers (past the approach to the Ravin de Balene, ignoring the gravel road at the tree) and continue for 8km to Venascle and the end of the tarmac road. From here a short drive along the dirt road brings you to a signposted footpath (GR4) that leads down left to a small valley that joins the main Val d'Angouire.

Easy going at the start of the Ravin d'Angouire

Descent

A level approach along the streambed leads to narrows and a pitch of 5m. Continue in increasingly impressive scenery, making a further nine or ten abseils until the gorge levels out, at which point there is a resurgence and a series of pools. A junction with the Ravin de Vénascle marks the end of the difficulties, after which the gorge opens out into wooded slopes. A path, then road, can be located on the right leading down to Beauvoir and the Chappelle St Pierre, the main road and your parking place.

Verdon area

Although crawling with tourists at Pointe Sublime and on the southern rim, it's easy to get away from it all in the incredible Verdon – often it's as easy as walking 100m from the road. Although canyoning is popular, the sheer scale of the place means that you are likely to enjoy a full wilderness experience if you go canyoning here. The Verdon Gorge can be usefully divided into three sections, **upper** (Point Sublime to La Maline, where there is a refuge owned by the Club Alpin Française), **middle** (La Maline to the belvedere at Maireste) and **lower** (Maireste to the Lac de Ste-Croix). The upper section (Route 36) is basically a gorge walk, while the middle section (Route

Canyoning in the Verdon? Check the water levels before you go!

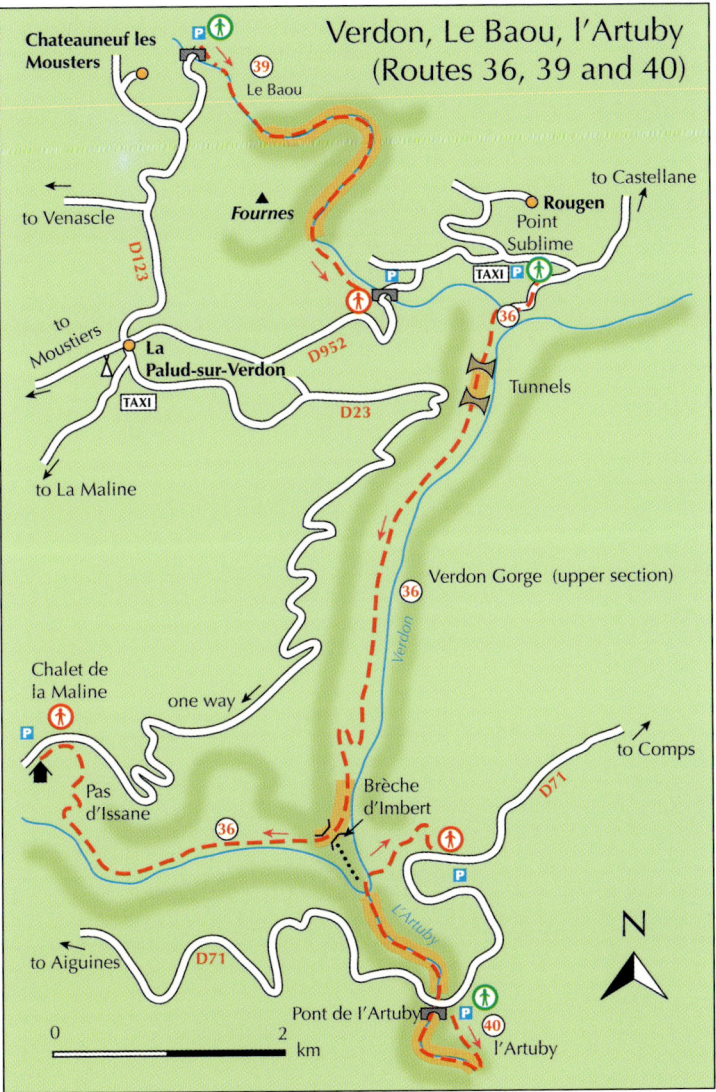

Verdon, Le Baou, l'Artuby
(Routes 36, 39 and 40)

Chateauneuf les
Mousters

Le Baou

39

to Castellane

to Venascle

Fournes

Rougen

Point
Sublime

TAXI

to
Moustiers

La Palud-sur-Verdon

D123

D952

36

Tunnels

TAXI

D23

to La Maline

Verdon Gorge (upper section)

36

Verdon

Chalet de
la Maline

one way

to Comps

Pas
d'Issane

Brèche
d'Imbert

D71

36

to Aiguines

D71

L'Artuby

N

Pont de l'Artuby

l'Artuby

40

0   2
km

37) is also easy for beginners and can be descended in its own right, although it often forms the return leg after descending one of the tributary canyons on the north side of the Gorge (Mainmorte, Font de Barbin, Ferne and Cabrielle – Route 38). The lower section is wide and easy, of no real interest to the canyoner and is often filled with small boats and pedalos coming from the Lac de Ste Croix. The Artuby (Route 40) is an area classic, very aquatic but no ropes required.

Water flow in the Gorge is regulated not just by the weather, but also by Electricité de France, who control a dam upstream and whose actions can dramatically increase the flow to dangerous levels. This does not affect the upper section but for the middle section and the side-canyons that finish within it, the rule is simple: **do not attempt if the water flow is greater than 6 m³/s (tel: 92 83 62 68).**

Access restrictions to wet canyons are often in place: May to October is the approved season but dates may change. Check with the Department of Tourism (tel: 04 92 31 57 29) or the National Park (tel: 04 92 74 63 95) for updated information. Dry canyons are not normally affected by seasonal restrictions, but a time limit of 10:00–18:00 normally applies.

36. Verdon Gorge – upper section **** 1

Length	10km
Descent	about 470m
Gear	torch
Season	all year
Time	5–6h
Map	IGN Gorges de Verdon–Moustiers-Ste-Marie 3442, 1:25,000

This is a gorge walk, easy going but a good length, with the added spice of ladders and tunnels. Not true canyoning, as you don't follow the watercourse at any point, but this walk is nevertheless not to be missed. (The downstream section, from La Maline to Mairesté, can be done separately; it is more serious and requires river-crossing and scrambling: see Route 37.) The walk can be done in either direction but here it is described north to south. Either way, you may want to arrange a taxi to pick you up at the other end. There is a taxi rank in La Palud, or taxis can be reserved by phone (06 07 65 19 49). Alternatively, try Taxi Verdon (06 68 18 13 13).

Approach

From La Palud-sur-Verdon take the road to toward Castellane (D952). After about 7km, either park at the Point Sublime, a well-known viewpoint for the upper part of the gorge, or continue for another 1km or so before taking a right turn, which leads to a dead-end parking area from where the walk begins (for those walking down from Point Sublime, a path shortcuts through the woods then along the foot of the band of cliffs under the Point).

Access point:
about 7km from La Palud

The high-level terraced path at Baume-aux-Chiens

169

Looking down to the Brèche d'Imbert

Descent

Five minutes' walk brings you to the base of the gorge. The path is obvious, and soon after beginning you pass through several long tunnels where a torch is essential. After the tunnels, look out for climbers on the right wall. There will probably be some teams on 'La Demande' – a notorious crack-climb that goes right to the top (about

400m). For the next few kilometres, the path is an easy woodland walk with the occasional rocky scramble and tremendous views. ▶

After some uphill zigzags, a series of steep metal ladders leads to the rocky little pass of the Brèche d'Imbert (about 3h30 to here). Past here, if desired, you can take a path down to river level at the point where the Artuby (see Route 40) joins the Verdon. Continue for about an hour to the Pas d'Issane, where the footpath (signposted Chalet de la Maline) leads up and out of the gorge (1h further) and welcome refreshment at La Maline. From here, try hitching or call to arrange a taxi.

Take care not to get sidetracked down to the river on one of the many minor paths.

37. Verdon Gorge – middle section *** 2

Length	about 8km
Descent	about 50m
Gear	wetsuit (or a shortie)
Season	all year
Time	5–8h
Map	IGN Gorges de Verdon–Moustiers-Ste-Marie 3442, 1:25,000

Mostly gorge walking, but plenty of aquatic sections – there are about 20 fords in this section. **Do not attempt if the water flow is greater than 6 m³/s (tel: 92 83 62 68).**

Approach

If you have two cars, leave one at the Col de l'Olivier above the lower Verdon. If not, you may want to arrange a taxi. Gain the Verdon's north rim road from La Palud and start at the roadside parking at La Maline. From here, follow the descent path to the gorge floor (40min).

Access point: about 10km from La Palud

Descent

The path is followed on the right side of the river for a few hundred metres to a footbridge (Passerelle de

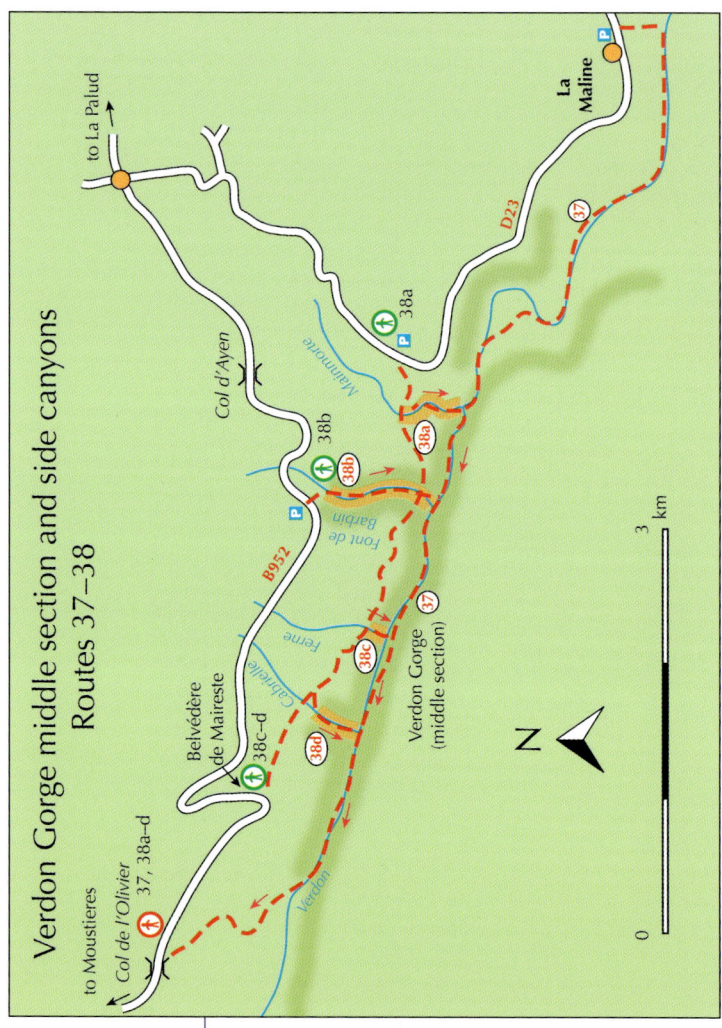

Verdon Gorge middle section and side canyons
Routes 37–38

l'Estrellier). Cross this and follow the path for about 2km until the gorge narrows. After an S-bend, the Ravin de

Mainmorte comes in from the right, followed by the Ravin de la Font de Barbin. About 3km further on, at the remains of a footbridge take the first right and head up the Col de l'Olivier and the road.

The steep walls of the Verdon's middle section

38. Verdon Gorge side-canyons: Mainmorte, Font de Barbin, Ferne, Cabrielle (all 4/4+)

Length	0.5–1.5km
Descent	200–450m
Gear	all the canyons are essentially dry, but you will need a wetsuit for the Verdon middle section. The exception is the last canyon, the Ferne, where water is normally more abundant. Rope, 2 x 50m minimum
Season	all year, but May to September recommended
Time	5–8h
Map	IGN Gorges de Verdon–Moustiers-Ste-Marie 3442, 1:25,000
Access points	about 6–10km from La Palud

VERDON GORGE SIDE-CANYONS	
Canyon	**Approach**
38a Mainmorte****	Sentier du Bastidon from loop road (20min)
38b Barbin**	Haute-Grau on the D952 (5min)
38c Ferne**	Belvédère de Maireste (D952), Sentier du Bastidon (45min)
38d Cabrielle**	Belvédère de Maireste (D952), Sentier du Bastidon (30min)

a Return time to the Col de l'Olivier or Belvédère de Maireste.
b If the water flow is less than 4m³/s, it is possible to head upstream to escapes at the

These four canyons are listed because of their reputation for high quality, although they have not been checked for this guide. All lie on the north side of the Verdon gorge, within easily reach from La Palud. The access points are on the La Maline road (38a, Mainmorte) or the La Palud–Moustiers road (38b, Barbin; 38c, Ferne; 38d, Cabrielle).

The routes are all are very committing, involve long free abseils (and, in the case of the Mainmorte, a Tyrolean) and should only be attempted by

Descent time	No of abseils	Return time[a]
3h	13	5h[b]
6h (escape possible on the Sentier du Bastidon)	17–21	3h
2h30	7	2h
3h	6	1h30

ughé (2h) or la Maline (3h30).

experienced parties and not at all (except perhaps for the Ferne, but you will still get wet) if the water level exceeds 6 m³/s (tel: 92 83 62 68). There are generally many short rappels as well as long, airy ones.

The Mainmorte is well-travelled; the others much less so.

All four of the routes emerge into the Verdon middle section (Route 37); descend this until an escape path leads up to the Col de l'Olivier. Here you could leave a second car or you may want to arrange a taxi.

The Verdon's placid middle-lower section has several steep tributary canyons

39. Le Baou ** 3 〰

Length	9km
Descent	230m
Gear	full wetsuit, rope (1 x 30m)
Season	May to October
Time	descent 5h, return 20min
Map	IGN Gorges de Verdon–Moustiers-Ste-Marie 3442, 1:25,000

This is a long canyon, mostly a wet walk at a higher altitude than the other Provence canyons, which gives a great expedition but can be cold and tiring. Full wetsuit recommended.

Access point:
about 5km from La Palud

Access

Take the D123 north out of La Palud-sur-Verdon for about 3km. At a wide bend, take a right fork leading uphill into woodland and drop down to the valley until you reach a tiny bridge (1km). Park here, where the stream disappears rather unspectacularly into scrub.

Descent

Follow the stream, hiking and wading, with long sections interspersed by short abseil pitches (five in all, with chains in place; Tyrolean after the fourth). Escape is possible at several points on the left bank. After a large meander around a minor peak (Fournes, 1139m), look out for a path on the right bank, which leads to the D952 between La Palud and Point Sublime. Taxi or hitch from here.

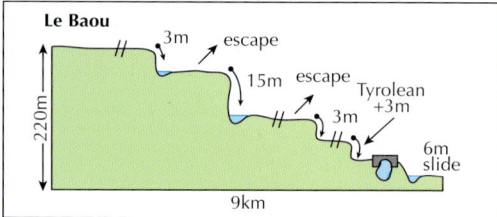

40. L'Artuby *** 3 ≋

Length	4km
Descent	50m
Gear	shortie
Season	May to September
Time	approach 30min, descent 4h30, return 1h
Map	IGN Gorges de Verdon, Moustiers-Ste-Marie 3442, 1:25,000

Lots of hiking, swimming and wading in usually cold water, with pools, boulders and potholes adding spice. In terms of obstacles, there are no pitches, just plenty of waterslides and some areas of big boulder chaos. The water level must be judged carefully, as the canyon is usually descended when there is not much flowing water, and **it becomes very difficult and hazardous in spate**. If the Verdon is flowing at a rate over 6 m³/s (tel: 92 83 62 68) due to spring meltwater or rainfall (as opposed to hydroelectric activity), go elsewhere. A great, atmospheric canyon.

Access

Start at the spectacular Pont de l'Artuby, east side, where there is ample parking and a good view of the canyon below. Head south over scrubby ground on a path, level at first, that eventually snakes down to the canyon floor.

Access point:
about 1hr drive from La Palud or Moustiers

Descent

Follow the bed of the canyon through the narrows, with some long swimming sections in static water, to meet cold, flowing water that originates underground. Continue into a more open and sunny downstream section with *marmites* and other erosion features, passing under the Pont de l'Artuby, continuing to a junction with the Verdon. To escape, cross the Verdon and head upstream for 300m and then cross again to a beach on the other side, from where a marked pathway leads to the D71 at Balcon de la Mescla. From here, an easy walk leads back to the Pont l'Artuby parking area.

ITALY

In the canyons of your mind
I will wander through your brain
To the ventricles of your heart, my dear
I'm in love with you again

Viv Stanshall

Italy has huge potential for canyon development and some of this has come to fruition in recent years in regions such as Liguria and the islands of Sicily and Sardinia. Due to its attraction for English-speaking climbers and walkers, Sardinia is the region covered in this book. In Sardinia, there is easily enough good casual canyoning to distract the climber or walker looking for a break from their normal activity, and even enough canyoning to make a week's dedicated trip worthwhile.

SARDINIA

Sardinia, at about 270km by 145km, is the second largest island in the Mediterranean. It is situated directly to the south of Corsica, from which it is separated by only a few kilometres. Although other parts of the island are well-populated, the eastern side of Sardinia is the location of some of the Mediterranean's most beautiful and interesting landscapes, with rocky peaks and soaring cliffs contrasting with isolated coastal coves, crescent beaches and intriguing ancient ruins of the Nuragic civilisation. The area of interest to canyoners is in the area south of Nuoro, in the semi-wilderness of the rugged limestone hills. The area is enclosed by the National Park of Golfo di Orosei et del Gennargentu. Close by are the coastal cliffs of Cala Gonone, where there is excellent sport-climbing.

Although Italian is the official language in Sardinia, the ancient tongue of Sardo is widely spoken and centuries of Spanish rule have also had an impact especially in the Alghero area where a Catalan dialect has survived.

Practicalities
Getting there
Easyjet fly from Gatwick to Olbia (March to October) and from Luton to Cagliari (March to September); Ryanair operate from Stansted, Liverpool and East

Midlands to Alghero; and Meridiana also offer Gatwick to Olbia on occasion. You can also fly to Tortolì/Arbatax in summer (May to October) but you would have to change in Milan, Germany or Switzerland. Try Air Dolomiti, Air Alps or ClubAir.

Flight time is generally about 2h30 and a car journey from Alghero airport or Cagliari airport to the Dorgali/Cala Gonone area will take 3–4h.

When to go
Canyoning is possible all year. Most of the canyons are essentially dry all year round and wetsuits are not needed but where water sections such as pools and slides occur they will be very cold in the winter and early spring.

Getting around can be exciting at Cala Gonone

Where to stay

There is lots of accommodation in the Nuoro and Dorgali area during the season, and some apartments and villas are now being hired at good off-season rates. Accommodation in the form of apartments and hotels is plentiful in the seaside tourist resort and climbing centre of Cala Gonone. For self-catering apartments here try contacting Tiziana Marongiu (matizia@tiscalinet.it). The Cala Gonone campsite, which is well-situated but can be noisy, has full facilities and is open from Easter to September (Via Collodi 1, tel: (+39) 784 93165, fax: (+39) 784 93255, www.campingcalagonone.it). There is year-round camping at the Refugio

SARDINIA ROUTES	Grade	Quality	Rock	Length (km)	Des (r
41. Codula Fuili	2+	*	L	3.0	3
42. Riu Gorropu	1+	***	L	1.5	
43. Riu Fluminedde and Golade Gorropu	4+HS	***	L	6.0	1.
44. Codula Orbisi	4 〰	***	L	1.0	2
45. Badde Pentumas	3-	***	L	2.5	4
L – limestone					

Bear Rock: a granite taster of Corsica just across the water

Monte Maccione near Oliena (about 45min from Cala Gonone). Follow the signs to Ennis from Oliena. The Refugio has a bar and restaurant. In Isili, the *auberges* in the town provide excellent good value accommodation. Here, and in Domusnòvas, there are several possibilities for free camping.

Getting around

If you arrive in Alghero or Porto Tórres, the fastest way to reach the Dorgali and Cala Gonone area is on the SS131 past Sassari and down to Macomer, then to Nuoro on the SS129 and then the SS131 to the branch to Dorgali and Cala

...ason	Time	Gear (optional/seasonal)	Access
...year	2.30–4.00	Rope	1–2 cars or walk from Cala Gonone
...year	5.30	-	car
...year	9.00	Rope (wetsuit)	2 cars
...year	7.30	Rope, wetsuit	car
...year	7.00	Rope	car

Gonone. From Cágliari, the fastest route is the SS131 to Nuoro. The SS125 from Cágliari to Cala Gonone is scenic, long and slow. Unless your activities are centred on the crags and footpaths around Cala Gonone, a car is essential. If you choose to use public transport, Dorgali is served by regular buses from other island towns and there is a service from Dorgali to Cala Gonone harbour (timetable information: tel: (+39) 800 865 042, www.arst.sardegna.it). The island's rail network does not extend to the canyoning areas or their environs.

Maps and guides
General maps for getting around the island include the handy Insight Travel 1:300,000 map. The relevant Instituto Geografico Militar (IGM) 1:50,000 maps to the area are 500 (Nuoro Est) for Badde Pentumas, Cala Gonone and Codola Fuili and 517 (Baunei) for the Gorropu area. Canyoning, climbing and walking guides are available in local newsagents and in the Bar La Pineta in Cala Gonone. Useful web resources for Sardinian canyoning can be found at www.descente-canyon.com, www.barranquismo.net/buscador/italia.htm and www.segnavia.it/canyoning.

Mountain rescue
For emergency services in Sardinia call 118. Mountain rescue teams can be alerted using this number and despatched by helicopter as required.

Other activities
Hiking and rock-climbing are the other major attractions in the well-known Cala Gonone area. For these activities, the *Rother Walking Guide: Sardinia*, and the English edition of Maurizio Oviglia's climbing guide *Pietra de Luna* (Fabula) are invaluable. The Nuragic villages are worth visiting; there are several good ones near Nuoro. They feature complex arrangements of circular huts dating back to the Bronze age. Tiscali has a different origin – built inside a cave inside Monte Corrasi are clusters of walled huts that were inhabited until a relatively late period, leading to speculation that the residents were in hiding from the Romans.

THE ROUTES

The Sardinian canyons are a varied bunch, but always impressive. The Goroppu (Route 42) is a spectacular gorge walk, which (once past the long approach) is eminently suitable for beginners or an easy day, as you can turn back if things get too tricky. The Fuili (Route 41) would make a good introduction to canyoning for someone competent at abseiling, while the remaining canyons are longer, more technical, and more spectacular, Badde Pentumas (Route 45) being a personal favourite. All are formed from finest Dolomitic limestone.

*41. Codula Fuili * 2*

Length	3km
Descent	340m
Gear	1 x 40m rope
Season	January to December
Time:	approach 0h, descent 2h30, return 5min plus 11km by road; or a steep 45min hike back to the road and a 1km level road walk.
Map	IGM 500 II Dorgali, 1:50,000

This is a dry descent. This gorge, with its modest but interesting scale and short abseils, gives a very good introductory trip. The scenery increases in grandeur in the lower section, past all difficulties, as one approaches the coastal cove of Cala Fuili, which is accessible by road and is very popular with climbers.

Access
From Cala Gonone, take the main road toward Dorgali (SP26) for a few kilometres. Just past the first hairpin bend take a left turn signposted Nuraghe Mannu. The narrow road contours the hillside, with the canyon emerging on the left as you pass over a shoulder. At

Access point:
about 10km from Dorgali

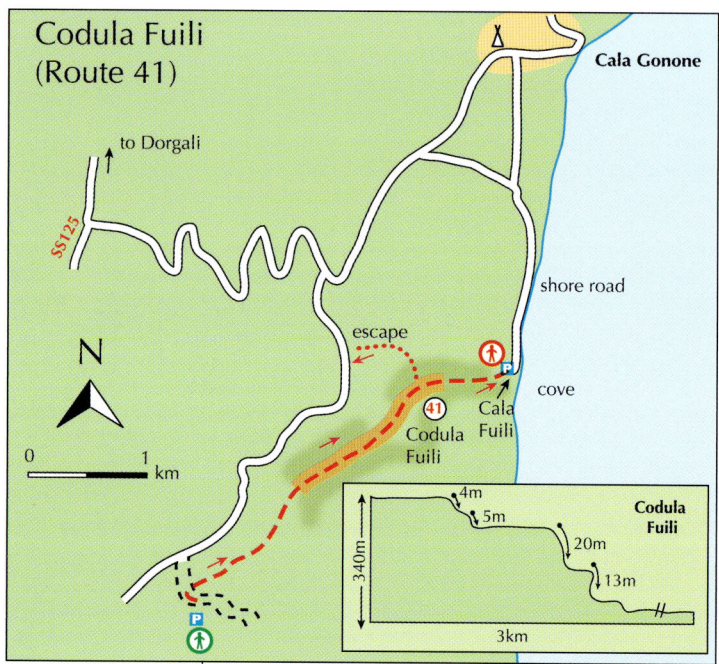

Codula Fuili
(Route 41)

to Dorgali

SS125

escape

shore road

Cala Fuili

cove

N

0   1 km

41
Codula
Fuili

Cala Gonone

Codula Fuili

4m
5m
20m
13m

340m

3km

about 5km there is a junction. Take the left fork that leads
down to a parking area at the head of the gorge, which is
very open and ill-defined at this point. If you have a second vehicle, leave it at Cala Fuili.

Descent
Follow tracks through pleasant meadows until a couple
of short rock steps bar the way (abseil point on the right).
The steps can be tackled in one pitch, or split at a stance
on the commodious halfway ledge; either way, take care
not to swing uncontrollably under the initial small overhang. Now the streambed follows an increasingly rocky
course, and takes a right turn into a mini Gordale Scar,
with smooth walls impending over a gloomy interior.
Traverse the right wall, clipped into cables, to reach an

Rugged gorge scenery in the Codula Fuili

abseil anchor. At the bottom of the pitch, follow an impressive corridor to another pitch over a bulging dry waterfall. From here, a scramble leads to open gorge walking through lovely wooded glades to the cove, from where steep steps lead up left to the coast road.

Alternatively, if you don't have a second vehicle and want to avoid a long walk via the Cala Gonone shore road, you can regain the road and your car as follows. Reverse the last 600m of the gorge to the last bolted climbing crag on the right (known to climbers as Vigiani). Just past this is a fairly obvious tributary gorge that comes in a steep, straight line from the north. Ascend this by some very rough scrambling to emerge at the rim of the gorge by an imposing fence around some residential buildings. Skirt the fence to the left to gain the road overlooking the gorge. From here, an easy walk of about a kilometre leads back to the parking area.

42. Golade Gorropu *** 1+

Length	1.5km
Ascent/descent	80m
Gear	none needed
Map	IGM 517 IV Funtana Bona and 517 I Genna Silana, 1:50,000
Season	January to December
Time	approach 1h30, ascent and descent 2h30, return 1h30

A simple but exciting walk up the Gorropu gorge past one of the biggest limestone walls on the island, followed by some easy scrambling to a natural barrier higher up the gorge. There are fixed ropes in place on all the tricky bits. The impressive caves and hill fort of Monte Tiscali can be accessed from near the start, but visiting both the Gorropu and Tiscali would make a very long day.

Access point: about 15km from Dorgali

Access and ascent/descent
From Cala Gonone, take the main road toward Dorgali (SP26), pass through the tunnel, and turn left onto the

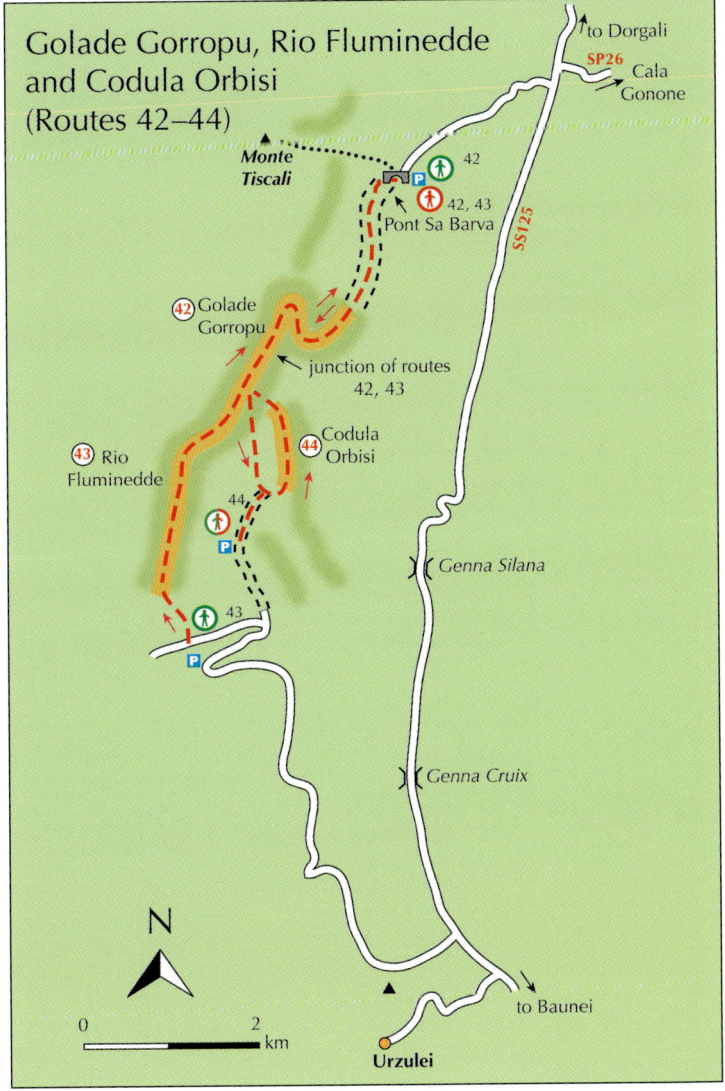

Golade Gorropu, Rio Fluminedde and Codula Orbisi (Routes 42–44)

Dorgali–Baunei road (SS125). After a short distance (about 1km), turn right and follow a twisting minor road for 9km, ignoring minor turn-offs and keeping the main valley more or less to your right, until almost reaching the valley floor. Continue along the valley heading south until a gash in the ridge opposite comes into view. This is the walking route to Monte Tiscali. Continue for 1–2km and park at a bridge (Sa Barva) in the base of the valley.

Now on foot, cross the bridge and take a left to walk south down the dirt road. At junctions, keep heading south along the valley on the main track, keeping parallel to the high ridge on your right. Ignore side-tracks to the left or right. After about 90min, enter the jaws of the Gorropu at a wooded glade. Here the situation changes dramatically as the gorge deepens. Continue up the wide riverbed in impressive surroundings, with a huge overhanging wall on your left. Fixed swarm ropes can be used to overcome three or four steep or smooth sections in the canyon bed. After about 1.5km you come to a dry waterfall, an insurmountable obstacle that marks the turnaround point (a steep scramble can be made to a ledge on the right, but a rope is then needed to make any further progress – better to come down Route 43 to this point!). Retrace your steps back to the gorge entrance, and then walk back to your car.

43. Riu Fluminedde and Golade Gorropu
*** 4+ (HS)

Length	6km
Descent	135m
Gear	1 x 45m rope, optional wetsuit, two cars (or a drop-off)
Maps	IGM 517 IV Funtana Bona and 517 I Genna Silana, 1:50,000
Season	January to December
Time	approach 15min, descent 7h, return 1h30 and 45km by road.

A long, rewarding descent that, depending on conditions and the state of fixed gear, may require some short sections of climbing at about Hard Severe grading. When last checked, some of the abseil anchors were bordering on inadequate, though later information indicates that these have been replaced. NB: This description has not been fully checked, and up-to-date information should be sought before embarking on this tricky descent.

Access

Head south from Dorgali on the SS125. After about 25km there is a minor road on the right, just the other side of a pass (Genna Cruix, 906m). If you meet a second junction with a right turn for Urzulei you have gone too far. Follow this tortuous road until the canyon appears as you go past a shoulder and begin to zigzag downhill. At a road junction you can choose between a left turn for the full canyon (park about 700m further on), or, for a slightly truncated version of the route, take the right fork in the direction of Sedda Ar Baccas (park after about 500m by a minor track on the left). Note that the canyon finishes a long way from your starting point, about 50km by road, and so two vehicles are ideal (see Route 42).

Access point:
about 1hr drive from Dorgali

Gorropu boulder-hopping under one of the biggest cliffs in Sardinia (Route 43)

Descent

For either descent, follow a north-easterly route into the canyon and follow the riverbed to a pitch of about 18m, followed by smaller pitch and a shallow water-slide (abseil anchor available) above a third vertical pitch that ends in a pool. After a fourth pitch and a boulder section, look for a steep little pitch of rock-climbing (roughly equating to a UK grade of hard severe, bolt runner) that gains a vegetated ledge on the right. This allows you to bypass a series of deep pools for which a wetsuit (or a dinghy!) is advised. A secondary gorge junction comes in from the right not far after this point. The next two drops of 5–6m can be bypassed on the left and right, respectively, and the underground pool can be abseiled direct or avoided by more devious means. A final pitch of 10m lands you at the head of the easily–accessible section of the Gorropu (junction with Route 42). Easy walking and scrambling (1h30) leads to the path, the Ponte Sa Barva (another 1h30) and (if you have planned ahead) your pick-up vehicle.

44. Codula Orbisi *** 4 〰

Length	1km
Ascent/descent	240m
Gear	2 x 40m rope, full wetsuit
Map	IGM 517 IV Funtana Bona, 1:50,000
Season	January to December, but cold in the winter months
Time	approach 15min, descent 6h30, return 45min

A deep and atmospheric canyon with plenty of water features including narrow channels and pools. The great scenery, old bolt anchors and long abseil pitches confer a relatively serious, but exhilaratingly remote, feel.

Access

As for Riu Fluminedde/Golade Gorropu, take the SS125 south from Dorgali and after 25km or so take a minor

Access point:
about 1hr drive from Dorgali

road on the right, just the other side of a pass (Genna Cruix, 906m). If you meet a second junction with a right turn for Urzulei you have gone too far. The road is metalled at first. The valley on the right, in its lower reaches, becomes your objective. Past a shoulder, the road zigzags downhill to road junction. Take the right fork in the direction of Sedda Ar Baccas and park about a kilometre further on. Continue on foot down the track for about 500m and drop into the gorge.

Descent

A couple of short pitches lead to a spectacular free abseil pitch of 35m that lands you in a pool. Passing a possible escape on the left at this point, scramble down to find another couple of pitches, separated by a 3m rock barrier. Avoiding the cave option, negotiate another 3m uphill pitch that leads to the final abseils. From the base of the final pitch (almost at a junction with the lower section of the Fluminedde gorge, which could be followed to the Gorropu if desired) escape up left to a ridge leading back south your parking place.

45. Badde Pentumas *** 3-

Length	2.5km
Ascent/descent	460m
Gear	50m rope, extra slings and krabs if you intend to do the *via ferrata* finish
Map	IGM 500 III Oliena, 1:50,000
Season	January to December
Time	approach 2h, descent 5h, return 15min

A fine canyon in a superb mountain limestone setting, with an interesting, if strenuous, approach walk. Well-defined abseil pitches lead down excellent features but nothing too intimidating and the anchors are good. This is essentially a dry canyon for most of the year.

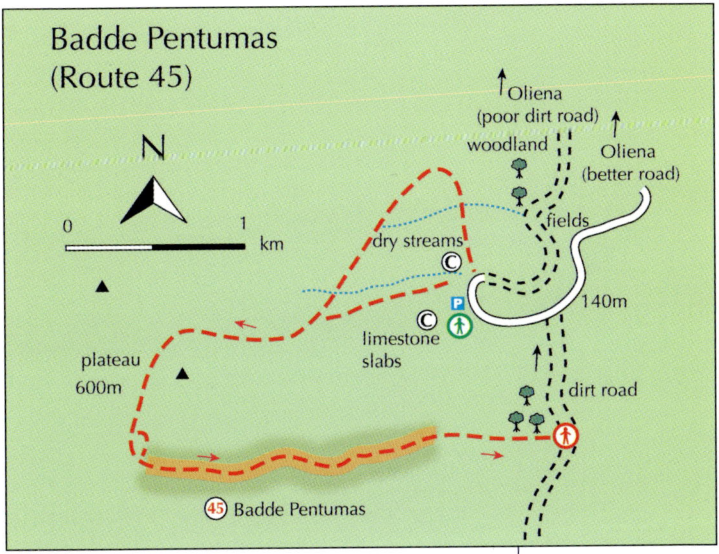

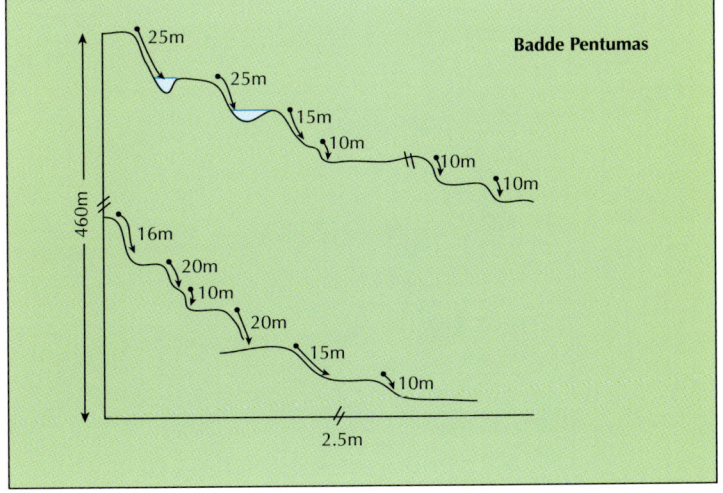

Badde Pentumas
(Route 45)

N

0   1 km

Oliena
(poor dirt road)

Oliena
(better road)

woodland

fields

dry streams

C

limestone
slabs

C

P

140m

plateau
600m

dirt road

45 Badde Pentumas

Badde Pentumas

25m

25m

15m

10m

10m

10m

460m

16m

20m

10m

20m

15m

10m

2.5m

Access point:
about 40min drive
from Dorgali

Access

Leave Dorgali heading north on the SS125. After about a kilometre, turn left in the direction of Nuoro, and, 4.5km later, turn left for Oliena. After about 8km, a kilometre beyond the second of two bridges, turn sharp left (sign-posted Grotta de Sa Oche). After 2km take a right turn (you have gone too far if you get to a chapel and a dead end) and follow a dirt road along the hillside. The road turns south into the Oche valley. Follow the left fork and park at an extensive layby near the caves.

Either take a footpath that heads north then doubles back to make a rising traverse of the hillside above, or, more direct, cut the corner by following the streambed for a few minutes, then heading up left to a series of slanting and enchanting limestone pavements that leave the path at about 475m (after an hour). Follow the path to a shoulder, where the terrain levels off somewhat. Pick up paths heading south (left) through meadows to a dry streambed and the head of the canyon.

Descent

The canyon starts in earnest with a 25m abseil into an amazing natural amphitheatre of white limestone. Skirt a pool on the right and abseil another similar pitch followed by a third, shorter pitch. Scrambling and walking sections, interspersed with pitches ranging from 8–20m, follow. ◄

Leaving the gorge behind, a short walk through scrubby valley terrain leads to the dirt road, which forms a loop hereabouts. Turn left and locate your car in a few minutes.

Although the grandeur of the scenery diminishes, interest is maintained right down to the foot of the canyon.

As an alternative, it is possible, some way after the fifth pitch, to access an exposed and reputedly worth-while *via ferrata* taking a ledge system on the right wall of the canyon (look for a way-marked scrambling and easy climbing route up ledges fixed with chains). This was created fairly recently by local enthusiasts; however, we were not able to locate the start of the route in 2004. Ideally, lanyards rather than cow's tails should be on your harness if you plan on doing this *via ferrata*.

Appendix 1
GLOSSARY

Technical terms

NB For full descriptions of canyoning equipment and techniques see 'Technical aspects of canyon descent'.

Abseil (or ab or rap) – controlled descent of a rope

Abseil device – a friction device such as a belay plate or figure-8 used for belaying and abseiling

Abseil pitch – steep section of canyon requiring the use of a rope for descent

Abseil station – an anchor used for abseiling

Aid – the direct use of fixed gear (eg bolts or slings) to make progress

Anchor – noun: a point of attachment such as bolt station, sling or tree used for abseiling or belaying; verb: to attach yourself to such a point

Belay – noun: a point of attachment such as bolt station, sling or tree used for securing yourself at the end of a pitch; verb: to secure a partner on a live rope as they climb or scramble, by locking the rope should they fall

Belay plate – a metal friction device that can be locked off to stop the rope passing through, used for belaying or abseiling. There are many designs usually known by their brand names, eg the Sticht plate, Tuber, Bug, Reverso and ATC

Bolt anchor – permanently fixed bolts, eg forming an abseil station

Bolt runner – a permanent runner placement, drilled and often glued, used for protection while leading a pitch

Breaking load – a force, usually a shock-load, sufficient to break or snap equipment

Cable traverse – a horizontal section using a fixed cable for handholds and/or protection

Committing – used to describe a manoeuvre that is impossible or difficult to reverse, such as a pulling the ropes after a steep abseil into an enclosed canyon

Cow's tail – a short sling clipped from the harness to an anchor or cable, enabling the canyoner's weight to be taken

Directissima – an unerringly direct line of ascent

Dynamic rope – rope designed to stretch so it can absorb shock-loading; used for lead rock-climbing or abseiling

Farmer John's – the inner piece of a two-piece wetsuit, looking almost like a pair of dungarees

Figure-8 – a) metal abseil device or b) secure knot used to belay, or to join ropes

Fixed rope or cable – a rope/cable left permanently in place to safeguard a difficult section

Free abseil – an abseil where you are hanging in space with no point of contact with the rock

Karabiner (or krab) – a metal link with a spring-loaded gate on one side. The gate can be of a locking design with an adjustable tubular sleeve to prevent accidental opening (locking karabiner; screw-gate karabiner) or not (snap-link or snap-gate karabiner). Used for connecting the rope, sling or harness to one another or to anchors, fixed cables, etc

Lanyard – used in *via ferrata* to describe the system for clipping into fixed cables etc, dual slings/ropes similar to cow's tails, but longer and with an added shock-absorbing device built in

Live rope – the active rope leading from a belayer to a leader or second

Maillon – a small chain link that locks with a screwing sleeve, often used on abseil stations to improve rope-pull

Pitch – section of a canyon needing an abseil descent

Prusik – noun: a sliding, locking knot used for ascending a rope or safeguarding an abseil descent; verb: to ascend a rope using such a knot

Quickdraw – a short sling with a karabiner at each end

Rappel/rap – see abseil

Reverso – a versatile type of belay plate that, in addition to its use in belaying and abseiling, can be reversed to give more friction on the rope, locked off automatically, or used as an emergency ascender

Rope protector – a piece of fabric placed over a sharp or abrasive edge to protect an abseil rope

Runner – protection placed when leading a pitch (short for 'running belay')

Scramble – easy climb requiring the use of hands, not difficult enough to be graded as a rock-climb, but still may require the use of a rope

Shock loading – sudden force exerted on a rope or belay

Shortie – a one-piece wetsuit with short sleeves and short legs

Shunt – a sliding, locking metal device used in place of a Prusik knot

Sling – loop of rope or tape, used for belaying, abseiling or for protection while roped-up

Squeeze – narrow section

Static line/static rope – rope with no capability for stretching and therefore no capacity to absorb a shock load

Swarm rope – a fixed rope used for hauling yourself up or down a short steep obstacle

Traverse cable – a fixed cable used for the hands and for protection

Tyrolean/Tyrolean traverse – a horizontal traverse along a free-hanging rope, anchored at both ends.

Geographical features

Aquatic canyon – a canyon involving swimming sections

Boulder choke – a pile of large boulders blocking the main canyon or passageway

Limestone – a sedimentary rock, composed largely of the mineral calcite (calcium carbonate ($CaCO_3$)). Limestone is partially soluble, especially in acid, and therefore forms many erosional landforms such as limestone pavements, potholes, caves and gorges

Conglomerate – a sedimentary rock consisting of rounded fragments of individual stones that have become cemented together

Dolmen – a type of single-chamber megalithic tomb, usually consisting of three or more upright stones supporting a large flat horizontal capstone; normally dating from the early Neolithic period (4000 BC to 3000 BC)

Labyrinth – a maze, usually found in a boulder-choke

Limestone spire – steep tower formed by erosion

Marmite – a smooth-walled, rounded pot formed by erosive water action

Pothole – deep cave

Siphon – an underwater current formed by a submerged passage

Stopper – the wave formed immediately downstream of an obstacle over which water is flowing; in the case of an overhanging or steep obstacle, the wave can form a trap

Sump – a short, submerged section of cave passage

Swirl-pot – a round, water-washed hole or chamber in the canyon floor; a *marmite*

Tufa – an unusual form of calcite rock, deposited in canyons and caves by calcium carbonate-rich water flow

Waterslide – a water-worn incline

Appendix 2
NOTES ON CORSICA

Corsica has dozens of well-documented canyons and would deserve extensive coverage in this book were it not for the fact that it is expensive and time-consuming to get to from Britain and the numbers of visitors from the UK is currently low. Nevertheless, a few details are given here for those interested in finding out more.

Getting there
Air France, AOM Airlines (01293 596663) and British Airways fly to Corsica via Paris from various airports in the UK. Southern Ferries sail from Nice and Marseille (see 'Introduction' for more details).

When to go
The canyons are mostly aquatic and April to September is the best season for good conditions.

The canyons
Most of the canyons are situated in the south, roughly between the western port of Propriano and the eastern towns of Solenzara and Porto Vecchio. The classics of the region include La Vacca, Piscia di Gallu and the Baracci, all of which are within easy reach of Bonifacio. There are also a few canyons in the Porto area.

Maps and guides
The island is covered by French IGN maps. Canyoning guides include *Corse, Paradis du Canyoning* (H Ayasse and P Dubreuil, 2001), and *Corse: 15 Canyons et 2 via ferrata* (JP Quilici, 2001). Useful websites include www.descente-canyon.com.

Appendix 3
INSURANCE, ACCIDENTS AND RESCUE

Travel insurance
Get travel insurance before you go. Consider British Mountaineering Council travel insurance (www.thebmc.com, tel: (0161) 445 4747). Take a European Health Insurance Card available in the UK from the NHS (www.nhs.uk) and check out health information (www.nhsdirect.nhs.uk, tel: 0845 4647 [24h, UK only]) and health-related travel advice (www.dh.gov.uk/travellers, tel: (+44) 20 7210 4850 [Mon–Fri, 09:00–17:00]).

Accidents and rescue
In case of an accident, make for the nearest habitation, call the emergency services (numbers below) and wait for their arrival. Use an accurately marked map or guide to describe the location.

The international distress signal is six blasts on a whistle or six torch flashes followed by a minute's pause, then repeat. The reply is three blasts or flashes followed by a minute's pause. Summon a helicopter by holding both arms in the air.

Emergency telephone numbers
Mainland Spain: Civil Guard and Mountain Rescue: 062. For the Guara area, Aragon SOS: 112; Aragon assistance 062.
Mallorca: There is no mountain rescue service on the island and if an accident

occurs or rescue is needed the Guardia Civil should be contacted (tel: 46 51 12).
France: Police: 17; Ambulance: 18.
Sardinia: Call 118 to alert the Protezione Civile, who will inform emergency services including local mountaineering rescue teams, who have access to helicopter transport.

Appendix 4
ACCIDENTS AND FIRST AID BASICS

This is a basic procedure for dealing with accidents, based on *Pocket first aid and wilderness medicine* (J Duff and P Gormly, Cicerone Press). Some of the steps below require previous skills training. Don't do anything inappropriate for your skills level.

1. Take control
- Stop, look, listen
- Consider whether you and the rest of the party are safe. If not, move or anchor yourselves.

2. Assessment and primary action
- Assess the mechanism of injury and whether the spine or head are affected. ***Drowning: perform CPR – see box below.***
- Talk and touch. Is the victim responsive? If they are conscious with normal breathing, go to 3.
- Is their airway open? If not, unblock it with a jaw thrust or lift.
- Are they breathing? Look, listen and feel – 10 seconds.
- If they are breathing with difficulty, give assisted breathing (mouth-to-mouth or mouth-to-nose)
- If they are not breathing, perform **CPR**.

3. Recovery position, bleeding and shock management

CPR
(CHEST COMPRESSIONS AND RESCUE BREATHING COMBINED)
5 assisted breaths followed by 30 chest compressions + 2 breaths. Repeat compressions at 100 a minute. Continue for 30 minutes.

- Unless spinal injury is suspected, put the victim in the recovery position so they don't asphyxiate on their tongue.
- Treat life-threatening bleeding (elevate limbs, direct pressure to wounds for more than 10 minutes).

- Rest and reassure the victim.
- Shelter the victim from wind, water and cold to prevent exposure.
- Relieve pain.

4. Secondary survey
- Does the victim have any relevant medical history?
- Head-to-toe physical examination
- Vital signs: record pulse and breathing rate every 15 minutes – this record is useful for subsequent medical assessment.
- ***Drowning: keep victim lying down until stretcher rescue.*** This applies even if they are apparently recovered.

5. Make a plan of action
- Administer any further treatment.
- Depending on the victim's injuries, get help or get the evacuation underway.

Appendix 5
CANYONS BY GRADE AND A TOP SIX

Below is a list of canyons in ascending order of difficulty/hassle/seriousness, based on various sources and personal opinions. (See 'Route grading and quality' in 'Technical aspects of canyon descent' for grade definitions.) You may disagree on the grades, depending on, for example, whether or not you are a strong swimmer or dislike long walks, but every self-respecting guidebook has a graded list, so here goes…

1 Véroncle, Gorges de
Verdon Gorge – upper section
Mascún Inferior, Barranco de
Gorropu, Golade
Pareis, Torrente de

2 Mascún Inferior, Barranco de – last section
Verdon Gorge – middle section
Opodette, Gorges d'
Opodette, Grand Vallot d'
Raboses, Barranco de les
Fuili, Codula
Balcés, Estrechos de
Notre Dame, Ravin de

2+ Estret de Peynes, Barranc de l'
Peonara Superior, Garganta de la
Vero, Rio
Balene, Ravin du
Barrasil, Garganta de
Relleu, Barranco de

3 Peonara Inferior, Garganta de la
Soler, Barranco de
Sant, Barranc del
Palomeras, Barranco de las
Formiga, Rio – Barranco de Yara
Valbelle, Gorges du
Infierno, Barranco del
Pentumas, Badde

Melo, Barranco de
Basender, Barranco de
Fornocal, Barranco de
Vénascle, Ravin de
Angouire, Ravin d'
Baou, Le

4 Portiacha, Barranco de
Biñeraix, Torrente de
Chimiachas, Barranco de
Balcés, Oscuros de
Ferne

Orbisi, Codula
Negras, Gorgas

4+ Mascún Superior, Barranco de
Cabrielle
Otín, Barranco de
Barbin, Font de
Mainmorte

5 Fluminedde, Riu
5/6 Gorg Blau, Torrente de and Sa
Fosca

A PERSONAL TOP SIX

- Riu Gorropu – rarely does a walk get so exciting
- Garganta de la Peonara Superior – hours of water-park fun
- Rio Vero – has The Boatman been this way?
- Barranco del Infierno – here be monsters!
- Oscuros de Balcés – the walls are closing in...
- Barranco de Mascún Superior – orchestral manoeuvres of every shade

Appendix 6
ROUTE SUMMARY TABLE

	Grade	Quality	Rock	Length (km)	Des (r
Sierra de Guara					
1. Rio Vero	2+ 〰	****	L	8.0	2
2. Barranco de Basender	3	**	L	0.6	1
3. Barranco de Portiacha	4-	**	L	0.25	1
4. Barranco de Chimiachas	4	***	L	1.5	2
5. Barranco de Fornocal	3 〰	***	L/C	3.0	1
6. Barranco de las Palomeras	3 〰	**	C	0.35	
7. Barranco de Mascún Superior	4+ 〰	****	L	2.5	1
8. Barranco de Otín	4+	***	L	0.5	2
9. Barranco de Mascún Inferior	1	**	L	3.5	
10. Barranco de Mascún Inferior – last section	2 〰	*	L	1.7	
11. Gorgas Negras	4 〰	***	L	4.5	1
12. Garganta de Barrasil	2+ 〰	**	L	2.5	
13. Garganta de la Peonara Superior	2+	***	L	4.5	1
14. Garganta de la Peonara Inferior	3 〰	***	L	2.5	
15. Oscuros de Balcés	4 〰	****	L	1.5	
16. Estrechos de Balcés	2	*	C	6.5	1
17. Rio Formiga – Barranco de Yara	3 〰	**	C	1.5	
Costa Blanca					
18. Barranco del Infierno	3 〰	***	L	1.0	
19. Barranc del Sant/ Barranco de Melo	1/3	/*	L	0.3/0.8	40/1
20. Barranc de l'Estret de Penyes	2+	**	L	0.3	
21. Barranco de Soler	3	*	L	800.0	3
22. Barranco de les Raboses	1+	*	L	0.3	
23. Barranco de Relleu	2+	**	L	0.8	1
Mallorca					
24. Torrente de Pareis	1+ 〰	***	L	6.0	1
25. Torrente de Gorg Blau et Sa Fosca	5/6	****	L	6.5	5

C – conglomerate, L – limestone

eason	Time	Gear (optional/seasonal)	Access
r–Oct	5hr30–6hr30 (one way)	-	2 cars or hitch/taxi from Alquézar
l year	2hr40	rope	car
l year	2hr30	rope	car
l year	6hr30–7hr30	rope	car
ar–Oct	5hr40	rope, wetsuit	car
l year	2hr40	rope, wetsuit	car
ay–Nov	7hr30–9hr	rope, wetsuit	walk fromRodellar
l year	6hr30	rope (wetsuit)	walk from Rodellar
ar–Oct	5hr15	(wetsuit)	walk from Rodellar
ar–Oct	3hr15	wetsuit	walk from Rodellar
n–Oct	8hr–10hr	rope, wetsuit	walk from Rodellar
ay–Nov	4hr30–5hr30	wetsuit	walk from Rodellar
ay–Oct	5hr30	wetsuit	1–2 cars
ay–Nov	5hr	wetsuit	car
ay–Nov	4hr30	rope, wetsuit	car
ay–Nov	5hr30	wetsuit	2 cars
ay–Nov	3hr15	rope, wetsuit	car
l year	4hr45–5hr45	rope (wetsuit)	car
l year	1hr30/2hr30–3hr30	rope/rope, wetsuit	car
l year	2hr30	rope, wetsuit	car
l year	3hr–3hr30	rope	1–2 cars
l year	1hr	rope	car
l year	3hr45	rope, wetsuit	2 cars
l year	4hr	-	1–2 cars
l year	8hr–10hr	rope, wetsuit, lamp	1–2 cars

	Grade	Quality	Rock	Length (km)	Desc (m)
26. Other canyons in the Sierra de Tramuntana	3–4	Up to ***	L	-	-
Haute-Provence					
27. Gorges de Véroncle	2	*	L	3.5	1(
28. Gorges d'Opodette	2	**	L	2.5	6
29. Grand Vallot d'Opodette	2		L	1.0	11
30. Gorges du Valbelle	3	**	L	5.0	35
31. Ravin du Balène	2+	*	L	0.5	5
32. Ravin de Riou	3	***	L	1.5	24
33. Ravin de Notre Dame	2	**	L	1.5	17
34. Ravin de Vénascle	3 ≋	***	L	2.5	25
35. Ravin d'Angouire	3 ≋	***	L	4.0	3C
36. Verdon Gorge – upper section	1	****	L	10.0	470 tot
37. Verdon Gorge – middle section	2	***	L	8.0	5
38. Verdon Gorge side-canyons:					
Mainmorte	4–5	***	L	1.5	7C
Font de Barbin	4–5	**	L	1.5	95
Ferne	4–5	**	L	0.5	70
Cabrielle	4–5	**	L	0.5	75
39. Le Baou	3 ≋	**	L	9.0	23
40. L'Artuby	3 ≋	***	L	4.0	5
Sardinia					
41. Codula Fuili	2+	*	L	3.0	34
42. Golade Gorropu	1+	***	L	1.5	8
43. Riu Fluminedde and Golade Gorropu	4+HS	***	L	6.0	13
44. Codula Orbisi	4 ≋	***	L	1.0	24
45. Badde Pentumas	3-	***	L	2.5	46

ª – Restrictions usually apply outside these months; L – limestone

ason	Time	Gear (optional/seasonal)	Access
year	-	rope, (wetsuit)	-
year	3hr45–4hr45	(rope)	car
r–Nov[a]	2hr15	rope (wetsuit)	car
year	1hr	rope (wetsuit)	car
y–Nov[a]	4hr30–5hr30	rope (wetsuit)	1–2 cars
y–Nov	2hr	rope (wetsuit)	car or taxi from Moustier
y–Oct[a]	5hr30	rope (wetsuit)	walk from Moustier
year	3hr	rope (wetsuit)	walk from Moustier
year	6hr	rope (wetsuit)	car or taxi from Moustiers
y–Nov[a]	5hr45	rope (wetsuit)	car or taxi from Moustiers
year	5hr–6hr	torch	car + taxi or 2 taxis from La Palud
year	5hr–8hr	wetsuit	car + taxi or 2 taxis from La Palud
year	8hr	rope, wetsuit	1–2 cars
st May–Sept)	9hr		or 2 taxis
	5hr15		from La
	5hr		Palud
y–Nov[a]	5hr20	rope, wetsuit	car + taxi or 2 taxis from La Palud
y–Oct	6hr	wetsuit	car
year	2hr30–4hr	rope	1–2 cars or taxi/walk from Cala Gonone
year	5hr30	-	car
year	9hr	rope (wetsuit)	2 cars
year	7hr30	rope (wetsuit)	car
year	7hr	rope	car

LISTING OF CICERONE GUIDES

BACKPACKING
Backpacker's Britain Vol 1 – Northern England
Backpacker's Britain Vol 2 – Wales
Backpacker's Britain Vol 3 – Northern Scotland
Book of the Bivvy
End to End Trail
Three Peaks, Ten Tors

BRITISH CYCLE GUIDES
Border Country Cycle Routes
Cumbria Cycle Way
Lancashire Cycle Way
Lands End to John O'Groats – Cycle Guide
Rural Rides No.1 – West Surrey
Rural Rides No.2 – East Surrey
South Lakeland Cycle Rides

CANOE GUIDES
Canoeist's Guide to the North-East

DERBYSHIRE, PEAK DISTRICT, EAST MIDLANDS
High Peak Walks
Historic Walks in Derbyshire
Star Family Walks Peak District and South Yorkshire
White Peak Walks Northern Dales
White Peak Walks Southern Dales

FOR COLLECTORS OF SUMMITS
Mts England & Wales Vol 1 – Wales
Mts England & Wales Vol 2 – England
Relative Hills of Britain

IRELAND
Irish Coast to Coast
Irish Coastal Walks
Mountains of Ireland

ISLE OF MAN
Isle of Man Coastal Path
Walking on the Isle of Man

LAKE DISTRICT AND MORECAMBE BAY
Atlas of the English Lakes
Coniston Copper Mines
Cumbria Way
Cumbria Way and Allerdale Ramble
Great Mountain Days in the Lake District
Lake District Angler's Guide
Lake District Winter Climbs
Roads and Tracks of the Lake District
Rocky Rambler's Wild Walks
Scrambles in the Lake District (North)
Scrambles in the Lake District (South)
Short Walks in Lakeland 1 – South
Short Walks in Lakeland 2 – North
Short Walks in Lakeland 3 – West
Tarns of Lakeland Vol 1 – West
Tarns of Lakeland Vol 2 – East
Tour of the Lake District
Walks in Silverdale and Arnside AONB

MIDLANDS
Cotswold Way

NORTHERN ENGLAND LONG-DISTANCE TRAILS
Dales Way
Hadrian's Wall Path
Northern Coast to Coast Walk
Pennine Way
Teesdale Way

NORTH-WEST ENGLAND
Family Walks in the Forest of Bowland
Historic Walks in Cheshire
Ribble Way
Walker's Guide to the Lancaster Canal
Walking in the Forest of Bowland and Pendle
Walking in Lancashire
Walks in Lancashire Witch Country
Walks in Ribble Country

PENNINES AND NORTH-EAST ENGLAND
Cleveland Way and Yorkshire Wolds Way
Historic Walks in North Yorkshire
North York Moors
South Pennine Walks
Yorkshire Dales – South and West
Walking in County Durham
Walking in the North Pennines
Walking in Northumberland
Walking in the South Pennines
Walking in the Wolds
Walks in Dales Country
Walks in the Yorkshire Dales
Walks on the North York Moors, books 1 and 2
Waterfall Walks – Teesdale and High Pennines
Yorkshire Dales Angler's Guide

SCOTLAND
Ben Nevis and Glen Coe
Border Country – A Walker's Guide
Border Pubs and Inns – A Walkers' Guide
Central Highlands: 6 Long Distance Walks
Great Glen Way
Isle of Skye, A Walker's Guide
North to the Cape
Pentland Hills: A Walker's Guide
Scotland's Far North
Scotland's Far West
Scotland's Mountain Ridges
Scottish Glens 1 – Cairngorm Glens
Scottish Glens 2 – Atholl Glens
Scottish Glens 3 – Glens of Rannoch
Scottish Glens 4 – Glens of Trossach
Scottish Glens 5 – Glens of Argyll
Scottish Glens 6 – The Great Glen
Scrambles in Lochaber

Southern Upland Way
Torridon – A Walker's Guide
Walking in the Cairngorms
Walking in the Hebrides
Walking in the Isle of Arran
Walking in the Lowther Hills
Walking in the Ochils, Campsie Fells and Lomond Hills
Walking the Galloway Hills
Walking the Munros Vol 1 – Southern, Central
Walking the Munros Vol 2 – Northern and Cairngorms
West Highland Way
Winter Climbs – Ben Nevis and Glencoe
Winter Climbs – Cairngorms

SOUTHERN ENGLAND
Channel Island Walks
Definitive Guide to Walking in London
Exmoor and the Quantocks
Greater Ridgeway
Isles of Scilly
Lea Valley Walk
North Downs Way
South Downs Way
South West Coast Path
Thames Path
Walker's Guide to the Isle of Wight
Walking in Bedfordshire
Walking in Berkshire
Walking in Buckinghamshire
Walking in Dorset
Walking in Kent
Walking in Somerset
Walking in Sussex
Walking on Dartmoor

UK GENERAL
National Trails

WALES AND WELSH BORDERS
Ascent of Snowdon
Glyndwr's Way
Hillwalking in Wales – Vol 1
Hillwalking in Wales – Vol 2
Hillwalking in Snowdonia
Lleyn Peninsula Coastal Path
Pembrokeshire Coastal Path
Ridges of Snowdonia
Scrambles in Snowdonia
Shropshire Hills – A Walker's Guide
Spirit Paths of Wales
Walking Offa's Dyke Path
Walking in Pembrokeshire
Welsh Winter Climbs

AFRICA
Climbing in the Moroccan Anti-Atlas
Kilimanjaro
Trekking in the Atlas Mountains

THE ALPS (Walking and Trekking)
100 Hut Walks in the Alps
Across the Eastern Alps: E5
Alpine Points of View
Alpine Ski Mountaineering
  Vol 1 Western Alps
Alpine Ski Mountaineering
  Vol 2 Eastern Alps
Chamonix to Zermatt
Snowshoeing: Techniques and Routes
  in the Western Alps
Tour of the Matterhorn
Tour of Mont Blanc
Tour of Monte Rosa
Walking in the Alps (all Alpine areas)

CROATIA AND SLOVENIA
Julian Alps of Slovenia
Walking in Croatia

EASTERN EUROPE
High Tatras
Mountains of Montenegro
Mountains of Romania
Walking in Hungary

**FRANCE, BELGIUM AND
LUXEMBOURG**
Cathar Way
Ecrins National Park
GR5 Trail
GR20 Corsica – The High Level Route
Mont Blanc Walks
RLS (Robert Louis Stevenson) Trail
Rock Climbs Belgium and
  Luxembourg
Tour of the Oisans: GR54 Walks in
  Volcano Country
Tour of the Vanoise
Trekking in the Vosges and Jura
Vanoise Ski Touring
Walking in the Cathar region
  of south west France
Walking in the Cevennes
Walking in the Dordogne
Walking in the Haute Savoie, Vol 1
Walking in the Haute Savoie, Vol 2
Walking in the Languedoc
Walking in Provence
Walking in the Tarentaise and
  Beaufortain Alps
Walking on Corsica
Walking the French Gorges

GERMANY AND AUSTRIA
Germany's Romantic Road
King Ludwig Way
Klettersteig Scrambles in
  Northern Limestone Alps
Mountain Walking in Austria
Trekking in the Stubai Alps
Trekking in the Zillertal Alps
Walking in the Bavarian Alps
Walking in the Harz Mountains
Walking in the Salzkammergut
Walking the River Rhine Trail

HIMALAYAS – NEPAL, INDIA, TIBET
Annapurna – A Trekker's Guide
Bhutan – A Trekker's Guide
Everest – A Trekkers' Guide
Garhwal & Kumaon –
  A Trekkers' Guide
Kangchenjunga – A Trekkers' Guide
Langtang, Gosainkund and
  Helambu – A Trekkers' Guide
Manaslu – A Trekkers' Guide
Mount Kailash Trek

ITALY
Central Apennines of Italy
Gran Paradiso
Italian Rock
Shorter Walks in the Dolomites
Through the Italian Alps: the GTA
Trekking in the Apennines
Treks in the Dolomites
Via Ferratas of the Italian
  Dolomites Vol 1
Via Ferratas of the Italian
  Dolomites Vol 2
Walking in the Central Italian Alps
Walking in the Dolomites
Walking in Sicily
Walking in Tuscany

NORTH AMERICA
Grand Canyon and American South
  West
John Muir Trail
Walking in British Columbia

**OTHER MEDITERRANEAN
COUNTRIES**
Climbs and Treks in the Ala Dag
  (Turkey)
High Mountains of Crete
Jordan – Walks, Treks, Caves etc.
Mountains of Greece
Treks and Climbs Wadi Rum, Jordan
Walking in Malta
Walking in Western Crete

PYRENEES AND FRANCE / SPAIN
Canyoning in Southern Europe
GR10 Trail: Through the
  French Pyrenees
Mountains of Andorra
Rock Climbs in the Pyrenees
Pyrenean Haute Route
Pyrenees – World's Mountain Range
  Guide
Through the Spanish Pyrenees GR11
Walks and Climbs in the Pyrenees
Way of St James – Le Puy to
  the Pyrenees
Way of St James – Pyrenees-Santiago-
  Finisterre

SCANDINAVIA
Pilgrim Road to Nidaros
  (St Olav's Way)
Walking in Norway

SOUTH AMERICA
Aconcagua

SPAIN AND PORTUGAL
Costa Blanca Walks Vol 1
Costa Blanca Walks Vol 2
Mountains of Central Spain
Picos de Europa – Walks and Climbs
Via de la Plata (Seville To Santiago)
Walking in the Algarve
Walking in the Canary Islands 1 West
Walking in the Canary Islands 2 East
Walking in the Cordillera Cantabrica
Walking the GR7 in Andalucia
Walking in Madeira
Walking in Mallorca
Walking in the Sierra Nevada

SWITZERLAND
Alpine Pass Route
Bernese Alps
Central Switzerland –
  A Walker's Guide
Tour of the Jungfrau Region
Walking in Ticino, Switzerland
Walking in the Valais
Walks in the Engadine, Switzerland

INTERNATIONAL CYCLE GUIDES
Cycle Touring in France
Cycle Touring in Spain
Cycle Touring in Switzerland
Cycling in the French Alps
Cycling the River Loire – The Way
  of St Martin
Danube Cycle Way
Way of St James – Le Puy to Santiago
  cyclist's guide

MINI GUIDES
Avalanche!
GPS
Navigation
Pocket First Aid and Wilderness
  Medicine
Snow

TECHNIQUES AND EDUCATION
Adventure Alternative
Beyond Adventure
Hillwalker's Guide to Mountaineering
Hillwalker's Manual
Map and Compass
Mountain Weather
Outdoor Photography
Rock Climbing
Snow and Ice Techniques
Sport Climbing

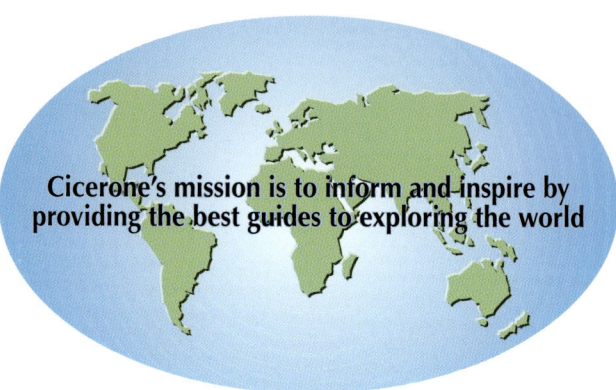

Cicerone's mission is to inform and inspire by providing the best guides to exploring the world

Since its foundation over 30 years ago, Cicerone has specialised in publishing guidebooks and has built a reputation for quality and reliability. It now publishes nearly 300 guides to the major destinations for outdoor enthusiasts, including Europe, UK and the rest of the world.

Written by leading and committed specialists, Cicerone guides are recognised as the most authoritative. They are full of information, maps and illustrations so that the user can plan and complete a successful and safe trip or expedition – be it a long face climb, a walk over Lakeland fells, an alpine traverse, a Himalayan trek or a ramble in the countryside.

With a thorough introduction to assist planning, clear diagrams, maps and colour photographs to illustrate the terrain and route, and accurate and detailed text, Cicerone guides are designed for ease of use and access to the information.

If the facts on the ground change, or there is any aspect of a guide that you think we can improve, we are always delighted to hear from you.

Cicerone Press
2 Police Square Milnthorpe Cumbria LA7 7PY
Tel:01539 562 069   Fax:01539 563 417
e-mail:info@cicerone.co.uk   web:www.cicerone.co.uk